The Book of Common Prayer and its Commentators 1655–1901

— DAVID JASPER —

ALCUIN CLUB COLLECTIONS 100

Sacristy
Press

Sacristy Press
PO Box 612, Durham, DH1 9HT

www.sacristy.co.uk

First published in 2025 by Sacristy Press, Durham

Copyright © David Jasper 2025
The moral rights of the author have been asserted.

All rights reserved, no part of this publication may be reproduced
or transmitted in any form or by any means, electronic,
mechanical photocopying, documentary, film or in any other
format without prior written permission of the publisher.

Every reasonable effort has been made to trace the copyright holders
of material reproduced in this book, but if any have been inadvertently
overlooked the publisher would be glad to hear from them.

Sacristy Limited, registered in England & Wales, number 7565667

British Library Cataloguing-in-Publication Data
A catalogue record for the book is available from the British Library

ISBN 978-1-78959-382-2

And I believe one Catholick and Apostolick Church. I acknowledge one Baptism for the remission of sins. And I look for the Resurrection of the dead, And the life of the world to come. Amen.

The Order for the Administration of the Lord's Supper or Holy Communion, Book of Common Prayer, 1662.

For
Bridget Nichols
with thanks

Contents

Abbreviations vi

Preface. vii

Introduction. 1

Chapter 1. Anthony Sparrow, *A Rationale upon the Book of Common Prayer* (1655). 7

Chapter 2. Hamon L'Estrange, *The Alliance of Divine Offices* (1659). 14

Chapter 3. Thomas Comber, *A Companion to the Temple* (1672–98). 21

Chapter 4. The contributions of the Antiquarians to the history of the Book of Common Prayer and its commentators: Joseph Bingham, *Origines Ecclesiasticae, or The Antiquities of the Christian Church* (1708–22); David Wilkins, *Concilia Magnae Britanniae et Hiberniae* (1737) 29

Chapter 5. Charles Wheatly, *A Rational Illustration of the Book of Common Prayer* (1710). 39

Chapter 6. William Nicholls, *A Comment on the Book of Common Prayer and the Administration of the Sacraments* (1710) 47

Chapter 7. Thomas Wilson, *A Short and Plain Instruction for the Better Understanding of the Lord's Supper* (1734) 53

Chapter 8. Richard Mant, *The Book of Common Prayer and Administration of the Sacraments . . . with Notes, Selected and Arranged* (1820) 61

Chapter 9. Charles Lloyd's unpublished Oxford lectures on the Book of Common Prayer (1823) 70

Chapter 10. William Patrick Palmer, *Origines Liturgicae* (1832). 77

Chapter 11. Edward Cardwell, *The Two Books of Common Prayer* (1839). 85

iv

CONTENTS v

Chapter 12. William Maskell, *The Ancient Liturgy of the Church of England* (1844) 93

Chapter 13. Francis Procter, *A History of the Book of Common Prayer* (1855) 106

Chapter 14. John Mason Neale, *Essays on Liturgiology and Church History* (1863) 117

Chapter 15. John Henry Blunt, *The Annotated Book of Common Prayer* (1866) 124

Chapter 16. The medieval roots of the Prayer Book: William George Henderson, *The York Missal* (1874); Thomas Frederick Simmons, *The Lay Folks' Mass Book* (1879) 133

Chapter 17. Walter Howard Frere, *A New History of the Book of Common Prayer* (1901) 141

Afterword: Towards G. J. Cuming, *A History of Anglican Liturgy* (1969) 150

Further reading **154**
Index **156**

Abbreviations

ASB *Alternative Service Book* (1980)
BCP Book of Common Prayer
EETS The Early English Text Society
LFMB *The Lay Folks' Mass Book*
ODNB *Oxford Dictionary of National Biography*
OED *Oxford English Dictionary*

(Note: The word "liturgy" is often used with respect to the form, or forms, of the Eucharist or service of Holy Communion. In the present book, it will be used in its wider sense to refer to the offices and services for public use, including the service of Holy Communion, in the Book of Common Prayer.)

Thanks to Bloodaxe Books for permission to use David Scott, "The Book of Common Prayer 1549" from *A Quiet Gathering* (1984).

The cover design incorporates a picture of a "chain" Prayer Book from Bramhall, dated 1737.

Preface

Lighten our darkness, we beseech thee, O Lord; and by thy great mercy defend us from all perils and dangers of this night; for the love of thy only Son, our Saviour Jesus Christ. Amen.

I must have said this lovely little prayer—the Third Collect for Evening Prayer—thousands of times since I was ordained as an Anglican priest in 1977. It can be found in the earliest of the versions of the Anglican Book of Common Prayer of 1549, but its origins are extremely ancient, drawing upon the Latin of the Gelasian Sacramentary of the eighth century, found in the order for Compline in the medieval Sarum (Salisbury) Use and, even further back, it is a paraphrase of the language of the Psalms. I last heard it said, or rather sung, at choral evensong in York Minster only a few days ago. At the end of the booklet provided on that occasion for the congregation by the Minster are the words, "This Order of Service is reproduced from *The Book of Common Prayer*".[1]

For more than half a millennium, the Prayer Book of the Church of England has provided the offices and liturgy whereby that Church has sung the praises of God, sought forgiveness of sins, made petitions to God and guided its people through the passages of life from birth to death. It was not invented by Archbishop Cranmer in the middle of the sixteenth century. Rather it is embedded in the ancient and medieval prayers of the Church, finding its central place in the Anglican liturgy of the English Reformation via the genius of Thomas Cranmer. The Book of Common Prayer is at the very heart of the identity of the Church of England, and this book will follow its history through some of the countless commentaries that have been written on the BCP from the seventeenth century until close to our own time. Close to, but not precisely, our own time. For perhaps my own generation is the last of the children of the Church of England who grew up with the Mattins and Evensong of the Church of England's Prayer Book as part of their weekly religious diet.

vii

Richard Morris, a contemporary of mine who, like me, was raised in an English vicarage in the 1950s, shares with me a sense that we are somehow close to the end of things in the Church of England that we knew—it is a time of evensong.

Morris writes:

> By any measure, parsons, parsonages and Anglicans are generally these days on the edge of things. Most of the older vicarages and rectories have been sold off, and surveys show that fewer than two in a hundred people go to Anglican services. Collapse has been generational. Few under forty now identify with the Church of England.[2]

This may be sadly all too true, and yet my book here is written as more of a celebration of the Church over the years—and a reminder of its real significance. Most of the names of the writers in the short sketches that follow are hardly familiar today. But many of them wrote books about the BCP that were, in their time, bestsellers, to be found on the shelves of countless rectories and vicarages and perhaps those of some layfolk as well. They wrote commentaries or books on the Book of Common Prayer and, in one case, lectures, that help us to understand our Prayer Book and its place in the ancient traditions of Christian worship and in our present spiritual lives. And their books were, in their time, widely read and appreciated in the Church that they served.

From its beginning, the Book of Common Prayer represented a vision of the Church that, arguably, started in 1549 and lasted through 1662 until the later years of the twentieth century, when the Prayer Book ceased to be the only authorized form of Anglican prayer and liturgy.[3] That vision of the Church of England as both "catholic and apostolic" underwrites this book. The men—and they were all men—who wrote these commentaries and scholarly books were also all Church of England clergymen, (except one—Hamon L'Estrange—who was a devout layman), writing in, for them, bad times and good. Most of them were men of deep learning according to their time. At the same time, they were not "academics" in the modern sense of that word. They were parish priests, bishops or deans of cathedrals, many of them serving the Church and its people with a pastoral care and devotion that was complemented by their scholarship. And all of them would have lived with the offices and sacraments of the Prayer Book every day of their lives. These brief essays will, I hope, be illustrative of a clerical profession that is at once pastoral, scholarly, theological and political. They were often far from perfect, as we shall see, but they were all men who said their prayers and those prayers were nourished by the Book of Common Prayer. They represent a scholarly, spiritual and pastoral tradition that is, perhaps, now fading from the Church of England—and to our cost. Mark Chapman has written in his book *Anglicanism: A Very Short Introduction* (2006):

> The 1990s saw efforts to make the archbishops into executive directors working through a board (the Archbishops' Council), which has failed to do anything to halt decline. Such managerialism sits uneasily with synodical and episcopal government. Whether the Church of England can any longer call on the passive support of a sympathetic majority in the multicultural society of contemporary Britain is an open question.[4]

But the present book is not about such managerialism in the Church. Amongst the authors whom we shall visit in the following pages, we find William Palmer, Francis Procter, John Henry Blunt and Thomas Frederick Simmons—hardly household names in the history of the Church—who all served faithfully and diligently for decades as parish priests while at the same time writing books of scholarly value about their Church.

The Prayer Book reminds us that no book comes to us *ex nihilo*. The same should be said, in a much more modest way, of this present volume. I encountered many of its authors for the first time when I was working with my former colleague from Glasgow, Jeremy Smith, on our book *Reinventing Medieval Liturgy in Victorian England* (2023). I owe a great deal to Jeremy and his deep learning. But also I have already admitted that which must be searingly obvious to any reader: everyone in this book is a man. The Church of England has been a deeply patriarchal institution for many centuries. Are there no women's voices that I have missed? Of course there will be those who tell me of the writers, both men and women, whom I have omitted, and in poor defence I confess that one always has to be selective, and selection leaves room for error.

But there are two women, both Anglicans, without whom this book could not have been written. The first is my wife, Dr Alison Jasper, whose critical but always creative understanding of the liturgy of the Church has been an endless source of inspiration. The second is Dr Bridget Nichols, lecturer in Anglicanism and Liturgy in the Church of Ireland Theological Institute, Dublin. Not only is Bridget's knowledge and understanding of the liturgy of the Christian Church both wide and deep, but she keeps me from despair by her boundless sense of humour and in her vision for the future—and without a vision, the people, and the Church, must surely perish. With Bridget around, I am sure, that will not happen.

Thanks are also due to the Drummond Trust for their generous support that made the writing of this book possible.

David Jasper
Glasgow
Feast of Bishop Gregory of Nyssa and his sister,
Macrina, Deaconess, July 2024

Notes

[1] The service was in commemoration of the 40th anniversary of the fire in the south transept of York Minster. I witnessed that terrible fire as it happened just as my father was about the retire as Dean of the Minster in 1984.

[2] Richard Morris, *Evensong: People, Discoveries and Reflections on the Church of England* (London: Weidenfeld & Nicolson, 2021), p. 1.

[3] *The Alternative Service Book* was authorized for use in 1980.

[4] Mark Chapman, *Anglicanism: A Very Short Introduction* (Oxford: Oxford University Press, 2006), p. 128.

Introduction

The essays that form the chapters of this book are largely, though not entirely, focused on what Geoffrey Cuming once described as "a new species of literature"[1] that came to life during the Commonwealth period in England in the middle years of the seventeenth century: that is, the "commentary" on the Church of England's Book of Common Prayer. By the time that Bishop Anthony Sparrow published the first of our "commentaries", his *Rationale upon the Book of Common Prayer* (1655), the Prayer Book was already more than 100 years old since its beginning with Archbishop Thomas Cranmer and the first Prayer Book of King Edward VI in 1549. Through its various revisions, it was to survive very largely unchanged in its essence until the present time, and it was not until 1980 that a wholly new book was authorized for use in the public worship of the Church of England—the *Alternative Service Book* (ASB), which even then was intended only as an "alternative" to the Prayer Book. The BCP was by then almost 450 years old, though rather less than that in its final 1662 form, and still authorized for use in the Church. Through all its many theological debates, the Book of Common Prayer has survived perhaps because it was just that—a book of prayer for common use—for our comfort and chastisement, for teaching, and to accompany us from birth to marriage and into death. As one modern poet, himself an Anglican priest, has described the Prayer Book of 1549:

This is just what you might expect
a Prayer Book to be like. This is
what we always thought about rain;
about dying, and marriage, and God.
We needed only the help which
the right placing of a relative pronoun
could manage. Words, then, said what they meant;
they bit. A man was a houseband
until death departed him.
And all was for common use:
printed in Fleet Street,
at the sign of the sun,
over against the conduit.[2]

The essays that follow, then, are not another history of the Book of Common Prayer and its various revisions at the hands of such figures as Bishop John Cosin or Bishop Robert Sanderson. Nor do they claim to be comprehensive. They can be read individually as brief insights into the individual writers and their books, the footnotes to be regarded as an important part of the text.[3] But taken as a whole, they are illustrative of the life of a book that has been at the heart of Anglican worship and theology since the Reformation, and illustrative in many different ways. Both Bishop Sparrow and Hamon L'Estrange, our first two authors, wrote their works under the dark cloud of the Commonwealth period (1649–60), when the public use of the Prayer Book was illegal. Sparrow, indeed, lost his Suffolk living of Hawkedon as early as 1647 for using the banned book in public worship. But by then the Book of Common Prayer was already ingrained in the sensibility of the national Church and its use never fully died out despite persecution. After the vicissitudes of successive reigns from Henry VIII until the Elizabethan Settlement, the writings of Richard Hooker (c.1554–1600), above all in the fifth book of his treatise *Of the Laws of Ecclesiastical Polity*, published in 1597,[4] established the authority of the Prayer Book. Thus it was that through the time of the Caroline divines (including Bishop Lancelot Andrewes (1555–1626), Archbishop Laud (1573–1645) and others), the Book of Common Prayer and its spirituality engaged the heart and

INTRODUCTION 3

mind of English culture, though not always without debate and fierce disagreement between the extremes of Puritanism and "Catholicism".[5] Hooker measured the Prayer Book against what he maintained were the first two tests of true religion, first "intrinsic reasonableness" and second the argument from antiquity. Dedicating his work to his old friend Richard Bancroft (1544–1610), the Archbishop of Canterbury, Hooker set out to defend the BCP against the accusation from Puritans that it contains too much superstition, and he strongly maintained that it is a book of pure devotion. Much the same might be said of Bishop Lancelot Andrewes, whose sense of the past and the tradition of the Church's liturgy was deeply held with reference to the spiritual life of the present. Later divines such as Bishop Jeremy Taylor (1613–67) made no distinction between doctrinal and devotional writing. Taylor's early work, *A Collection of Offices or Forms of Prayer in Cases Ordinary and Extraordinary: Taken out of the Scriptures and the Ancient Liturgies of Several Churches, Especially the Greek* (1657), though somewhat remote from the Prayer Book itself, was significant in its recourse to the authority of ancient liturgies, upon which later defenders of the Prayer Book laid such great stress.

These later Prayer Book commentaries and authors who will be our concern here wrote endlessly about the BCP, and, again, from a variety of perspectives. Some, like L'Estrange, were anxious to establish the primitive and patristic roots of the BCP. This obsession continues into the nineteenth century, as we shall see, when the Tractarians sought to establish clearly the "catholic and apostolic" credentials of the Church of England, in continuity also with English medieval traditions in the worship of the Sarum Use, the York Use, and so on. Others, like the saintly and much-loved Bishop Wilson of Sodor and Man, in his widely read and often reprinted *Short and Plain Instruction for the Better Understanding of the Lord's Supper* (1734), are profoundly pastoral in their concerns, seeking to relate the Prayer Book and its liturgy to the everyday lives of the people of his diocese, and in particular, as Bishop Wilson put it, "for the benefit of Young Communicants and of such as have not well considered this Holy Ordinance".[6]

The early decades of the nineteenth century and then later, in the heat of the Oxford Movement, saw a flurry of reprints of seventeenth- and eighteenth-century books on the Book of Common Prayer. The writings of Anthony Sparrow, Thomas Comber, Charles Wheatly and many others were reissued. Bishop Thomas Wilson and his writings were central to the series of *Tracts for the Times* (1833–41).[7] Hamon L'Estrange's practice of setting the different versions of the Prayer Book, together with the Scottish Prayer Book of 1637, in parallel columns was more fully developed by William Keeling in his *Liturgiae Britannicae* (1842), with the object "to exhibit the Prayer Book of the Church of England telling its own history".[8] Furthermore, as we travel further into the nineteenth century, we move somewhat beyond the immediate boundaries of the BCP itself, and to the concern amongst the Tractarians and others to establish the worship and liturgy of the Church of England firmly in succession to the rites of the longer Middle Ages, back to St Augustine of Canterbury in the early seventh century and even further. For them, looking back to Wheatly and others in the eighteenth century, the English Reformation was not so much a moment of discontinuity in the life of the English Church as a moment of repairing the corruptions of the later medieval period. It was a moment of continuity, and the worship of the English Church was essentially an unbroken chain of prayer and praise that reached back even as far as apostolic times. It is important then to include here the work of William Maskell in his *Ancient Liturgy of the Church of England* (1844), a significant comparative study of the Uses of Sarum (Salisbury), York, Hereford and Bangor together with the "Roman Liturgy", which begins with a reference to Cranmer's Preface to the 1549 Prayer Book and that which has been "corrupted" in the medieval Church's liturgy.[9] The growing volume of work on medieval liturgical texts in the nineteenth century, encouraged by such organizations as the Surtees Society, the Early English Text Society and, later, the Henry Bradshaw Society, is here represented by the work of William George Henderson and Thomas Frederick Simmons, both Anglican clergymen. Simmons, in particular, was deeply involved in the processes of Prayer Book revision in the later nineteenth century.[10]

The chapters here conclude with an essay on Bishop Walter Howard Frere and his extensive revision in 1901 of Francis Procter's *History of the Book of Common Prayer* (1855), a work that became widely and affectionately known simply as "Procter and Frere". If there is some

INTRODUCTION 5

continuity in Prayer Book studies between the middle of the seventeenth century and the end of the nineteenth century, then the twentieth century definitely saw a new era in the liturgical life of the Church of England. The report of the Royal Commission on Ecclesiastical Discipline of 1904 famously concluded that "the law of public worship in the Church of England is too narrow for the religious life of the present generation".[11] Change was necessary and the BCP, it was felt, was no longer up to the task for which it was intended. The next few decades of the new century saw the debacle of the "Deposited Book" of 1928, the development of new liturgies and prayer books in the worldwide Anglican communion, a growing ecumenism in liturgical scholarship and revision, and finally a wholly new prayer book authorized for use in the Church of England in 1980. All these things lie beyond the scope of the present work, which, it is to be hoped, will shed some light on the lively history of the Book of Common Prayer in the centuries when it was indeed the mainstay of Anglican devotion, prayer and sacramental life.[12] And so I end this brief Introduction with some more words of the priest-poet David Scott, describing an early morning service of Holy Communion "according to the book":

> ... we knelt where it advised us to,
> ungainly but meaning it, trusting to the words set
> (on paper difficult to separate)
> that what we did was acceptable.[13]

Notes

1   G. J. Cuming, *A History of Anglican Liturgy* (2nd edn, London: Macmillan, 1982), p. 112.

2   David Scott, "The Book of Common Prayer, 1549", in *A Quiet Gathering* (Newcastle upon Tyne: Bloodaxe Books, 1984), p. 36.

3   There is some deliberate repetition of material to allow readers to enjoy individual chapters as they wish.

4   Kenneth Stevenson remarked in his book *Covenant of Grace Renewed: A Vision of the Eucharist in the Seventeenth Century* (London: Darton,

6   THE BOOK OF COMMON PRAYER AND ITS COMMENTATORS

Longman & Todd, 1994), p. 36: "Hooker's writings left their mark firmly on virtually every Anglican theologian in the period after his death—and beyond."

[5] As Peter Marshall has pointed out in his history of the English Reformation, *Heretics and Believers* (London: Yale University Press, 2017), the term "Roman Catholic" was a relatively late development in the English Church, in distinction from an Anglican tradition that clearly saw itself as "catholic and apostolic".

[6] From the title page of Thomas Wilson, *A Short and Plain Instruction for the Better Understanding of the Lord's Supper* (1734).

[7] John Keble also wrote an extensive *Life of the Right Reverend Father in God Thomas Wilson DD* (Oxford: John Henry Parker, 1863).

[8] Preface to William Keeling, *Liturgiae Britannicae, or the Several Editions of the Book of Common Prayer of the Church of England* (London: William Pickering, 1842), p. iii.

[9] Cranmer's 1549 Preface, based on the preface to the reformed breviary of 1535 by Cardinal Francisco Quiñones, survives in the 1662 Prayer Book as what Maskell calls the "admonition" *Concerning the Service of the Church.* It begins with the familiar words: "There was never anything by the wit of man so well devised, or so sure established, which in continuance of time hath not been corrupted: As, among other things, it may plainly appear by the Common Prayers in the Church."

[10] See R. C. D. Jasper, *Prayer Book Revision in England, 1800–1900* (London: SPCK, 1954), p. 125, and David Jasper and Jeremy Smith, *Reinventing Medieval Liturgy in Victorian England: Thomas Frederick Simmons and The Lay Folks' Mass Book* (Woodbridge: The Boydell Press, 2023), pp. 119–44.

[11] Quoted in Cuming, *A History of Anglican Liturgy*, p. 163.

[12] The term "Anglican" is somewhat vague and is used here primarily with reference to the Church of England, recognizing that the situations in the United States and Scotland, for example, were rather different.

[13] Scott, "Early Communion", in *A Quiet Gathering*, p. 38.

1

Anthony Sparrow, *A Rationale upon the Book of Common Prayer* (1655)

It seems probable that Bishop Anthony Sparrow's commentary on the Book of Common Prayer, his *Rationale*, took its title from perhaps the most important and comprehensive of all medieval liturgical treatises, the *Rationale Divinorum Officiorum* of Bishop William Durandus of Mende (1230–96), written between the years 1286 and 1291.[1] Anthony Sparrow was born in Depden near Bury St Edmunds, Suffolk, in 1612 and received his university education at Queen's College, Cambridge, graduating with his BA in 1629 (MA, 1632). Ordained in Ely in February 1635, Sparrow, by then a junior fellow of his college, attracted the attention of Archbishop William Laud and gained some notoriety for his Laudian theological views, in particular for his sermon of 1637 entitled *A Sermon Concerning Confession of Sins and the Power of Absolution.*

Sparrow remained in Cambridge until 1644 under the protection of Laud, holding various university posts, including both Hebrew and Greek praelector, when he finally fell victim to the parliamentary purge of that university. In 1645, he married Susanna Orrell, and in September 1647 Sparrow became rector of Hawkedon, close to his birthplace of Depden. However, he remained there in office a mere five weeks, being removed from the parish for his illegal public use of the then banned Book of Common Prayer. It was this event that prompted the writing of his *Rationale upon the Book of Common Prayer of the Church of England*, first published anonymously in 1655. Within two years, the *Rationale* was reprinted with Sparrow's name on the front page as 'Anth. Sparrow B. D. sometime Fellow of Queens Col. Cambr'.[2] There were at least eight

7

8   THE BOOK OF COMMON PRAYER AND ITS COMMENTATORS

more editions published before Sparrow's death in 1685. The *Rationale* was later reprinted in the nineteenth century.

At the Restoration of the monarchy in 1660, Sparrow was reinstated to office in the church as the rector of Hawkedon, was elected to a preachership at Bury St Edmunds, and finally appointed to the archdeaconry of Sudbury. He became a canon of Ely Cathedral in 1661, recovering, with some distinction, his connections with the University of Cambridge as Master of his old college, Queen's, and as vice-chancellor of the university in 1664–5. Sparrow was then consecrated Bishop of Exeter in 1667, and translated to become Bishop of Norwich in 1676, where he died nine years later. Like his fellow East Anglian Hamon L'Estrange, as we shall see in the next chapter, Bishop Sparrow found himself caught between the extreme criticisms of both Puritans and High Churchmen, as he put it, "some clamouring loud against me for prosecuting schismatics, and some who profess great loyalty and zeal for the church, as loud complaining because we do not proceed violently beyond the rule of law".[3] Sparrow died in his episcopal palace in Norwich on 19 May 1685.

Sparrow's *Rationale upon the Book of Common Prayer* is notable for a number of reasons. My own copy of the 1657 edition is pocket-sized, perhaps for easy concealment, but expensively leatherbound and beautifully printed, an original metal clasp for the cover now missing. It begins with a list of the "Compilers of the *Common-Prayer Book* of the Church of England" of 1549, starting with Archbishop Cranmer and including the names of Bishops Goodrick (Ely), Ridley (Rochester) and others, all under the title "Doctor". The list ends with a quotation from King Charles' *Meditation 16 upon the Ordinance against the Book of Common Prayer*: "Hardly can the pride of those men that study Novelties, allow former times any share or degree of Wisdom or Godliness." Much of the *Rationale* that follows will be concerned with establishing the antiquity and apostolic credentials of the BCP. The Prayer Book is no "novelty". After a brief Preface, there are full-page portraits of Richard Hooker, Bishop Lancelot Andrewes and Bishop John Overall, the latter being a predecessor of Sparrow as Bishop of Norwich.[4]

Sparrow's Preface sets out to establish the authority of the BCP on two fundamental and sound principles, following the earlier lead of Richard Hooker—namely antiquity and reason. First, he affirms, "it [the Prayer

Book] is agreeable to Primitive usage", and second it is "a reasonable service and so not superstitious".[5] The Prayer Book is often attacked on two diametrically opposed fronts, Sparrow suggests: first, that it is merely "old superstitious Roman dotage", and second, that it is "schismatically new". As he takes a middle course, he affirms that neither extreme is true. He also emphasizes the scriptural basis of the BCP, finally ending his Preface on a pastoral note that characterizes the whole book. Indeed, Sparrow writes with a warmth that is almost entirely lacking in the more scholarly work of the layman L'Estrange, and it is Sparrow's pastoral concern as an incumbent and as a bishop that lies at the heart of his defence of the fixed and established liturgical forms and words of the BCP. He concludes his Preface with these words:

> How many millions of poor soules are in the world; ignorant, infirm by nature, age, accidents, (as blindness, deafness, loss of speech, etc.) which respectively may receive help by SET FORMS, but cannot so well (or not at all) by extemporary voluntary effusions, and then upon all these will build what he reads in this Book; he will, if not be convinced to joyn in Communion with, yet perhaps be so sweetned, as more readily to pardon those, who still abiding in their former judgements, and being more confirmed hereby, do use THE ANCIENT FORM.

There is indeed a gentleness about Sparrow's writing and form of argument that is often lacking in the often testy and acerbic rigours of seventeenth-century religious debate.

Contemporary references to seventeenth-century writings in the *Rationale* are relatively sparse after the Preface and its portraits, though one name does appear with some frequency: that of his near contemporary and fellow East Anglian, Herbert Thorndike (1598–1672),[6] and his principle work *Of Religious Assemblies and the Public Service of God* (1642), a defence of the Church of England against the Puritans in which Thorndike insists above all on the apostolic foundations of the Church's episcopal governance and its Prayer Book.

But Sparrow's primary resources in his defence of the BCP are patristic and, above all, the writings of St John Chrysostom and St

10   THE BOOK OF COMMON PRAYER AND ITS COMMENTATORS

Augustine of Hippo. Drawing together the worship of the Church from the earliest times until the present, he emphasizes the principle of unity: "How admirable a thing Unity—Unity in time, form etc. is."[7] In short, the Church is united in prayer throughout all ages. In the substance of his book, Sparrow takes his reader systematically through the text of the Prayer Book in clear and elegant prose which is still remarkably readable. He concludes with an extended essay on the architecture and ornaments of the Church entitled "Of Chancels, Altars, Fashion of Churches",[8] following the allegorical and symbolic method of his great predecessor Durandus. His approach to the church building is essentially conservative—nothing is to be changed from times past:

1. The fabric of the church is in the form of a ship, for "we were in this world as in a Sea, tossed and hurried with the troublesome waves and boisterous winds of diverse temptations" (p. 373).
2. "The whole church is a type of heaven" (p. 374)—Sparrow quotes Genesis 28:17, Jacob's words at the end of his dream of the heavenly ladder.
3. "The Nave or body resembles the lowest visible heaven or Paradise" (p. 375).
4. For the chancel (or, more properly, sanctuary), Sparrow offers no specific images but describes in detail its ornaments and purpose: "The Bishop sitting in this Seat by the Altar (having his assistant Priests sitting with him), resembles Christ, (with his Apostles by him) instituting the holy Sacrament, and blessing the prayers offered up at the Altar by the Priest; Right under this Seat stood the *Altar or Holy Table*, the Propitiatory, Christs Monument and the Tabernacle of his glory. The shop of the great Sacrifice." (pp. 378–9).

Sparrow is eager to affirm that no one should take offence at the term "altar" or the term "priest" (arguing from the Latin and the Greek). Finally he provides a scholarly account of the translation of the psalms in the BCP, defending the retention of the translation of Miles Coverdale, which "was doubtlesse out of the Hebrew". (We might recall that Sparrow was the Hebrew praelector in Cambridge from 1638–9). In an interesting note on the art of translation, Sparrow comments that the translation from the Hebrew is not always exact, "yet it holds to the sense and scope more than some suppose it doth, and many times much more than those who would seem to stick so close to the Letter".[9]

Sparrow was a capable theologian, and his discussion of the daily office, especially the office of Morning Prayer, is particularly significant in the outlining at some length of its theological structure. He then embarks on an extended commentary on the church's liturgical year, followed in the collects and readings set from the first Sunday in Advent. Perhaps surprisingly, and in contrast to Hamon L'Estrange, Sparrow's remarks on the Communion service are relatively brief following, without a great deal of comment, the text of the Elizabethan Prayer Book of 1559 and emphasizing the pastoral need for frequent communion. Using the authority of St Chrysostom and St Cyril, Sparrow establishes "the presence of Christ" in the "Consecration [which] consists chiefly in rehearsing the words of our Saviours Institution, This is my body, and this is my blood, when the Bread and Wine is present upon the Communion table."[10] Of the nature of the "real presence" in the Eucharist, Sparrow says little more, but he proposes a minimum of three communions for each parishioner in the year.[11] He concludes his discussion of Holy Communion with his only use of the term "sacrifice" in the whole of the *Rationale*:

> The Priest offers up the Sacrifice of the holy Eucharist, or the Sacrifice of praise and thanksgiving for the whole Church, as in all old Liturgies it is appointed, and together with that is offered up that most acceptable Sacrifice of ourselves, souls, and bodies devoted to God's service.[12]

The sacrifice is not Christ's alone but something in which we also share in our devotion to God's service. As authorities for this he cites St Augustine's *De Civitate Dei*, Book 10, Chapter 6[13] and Romans, Chapter 12, verse 1.[14]

A brave statement on its first publication in a highly dangerous age, Sparrow's deeply pastoral as well as learned and intelligent work was widely read after the Restoration, when it was frequently reprinted with the "Caution to his Diocese against False Doctrines", his first episcopal visitation charge to the clergy of the diocese of Exeter in 1669. A companion volume to the *Rationale* entitled *A Collection of Articles, Injunctions, Canons of the Church of England* was published in 1661. Sparrow's work might have disappeared from sight but for the renewed interest in the BCP in the nineteenth century. In 1839, using a copy of the *Rationale* printed in 1684, John Henry Newman edited a new edition, his work being again reprinted in 1843 and 1852.[15] The *Rationale* has not been reprinted since then.

Notes

[1]   The first book of Durandus' work became a key text in the ecclesiology of the nineteenth century in the translation by John Mason Neale (see Chapter 14) and Benjamin Webb, given the title *The Symbolism of Churches and Church Ornaments* (1843). There is a recent translation of the Prologue and Book One of the *Rationale* by Timothy M. Thibodeau (New York: Columbia University Press, 2007).

[2]   My own copy is dated 1657, printed in London, and is ascribed to Sparrow. On the title page, it directs that copies "are to be sold by T. Garthwait at the little North-door of St. Pauls".

[3]   Bishop Anthony Sparrow, quoted in John Spurr, *The Restoration Church of England, 1646–1689* (New Haven: Yale University Press, 1991), p. 82.

[4]   Bishop John Overall (1560–1619) was responsible for the section on the sacraments in the Catechism of the BCP. He was also one of the translators of the King James Bible.

[5]   Anthony Sparrow, *A Rationale upon the Book of Common Prayer* (London, 1657), Preface. The pages of the Preface are not numbered.

[6]   Herbert Thorndike was, like Sparrow, a Cambridge-educated churchman and theologian. He was also deprived of office under the Commonwealth, but reinstated in 1660, becoming a Canon of Westminster in 1661. Thorndike's work was eagerly read by the Tractarians in the nineteenth century.

[7]   Ibid., Preface.

[8]   Sparrow, *Rationale*, pp. 372–85.

[9]   Sparrow, *Rationale*, p. 399.

10 Ibid., pp. 270–1. The debate over the actual moment and words of consecration persists. In 1928, Evangelicals and Anglo-Catholics agreed on the "Western" view that consecration was effected by the recital of the Words of Institution, despite Bishop Frere arguing that in the primitive Church it was the whole prayer that was regarded as consecrating. See G. J. Cuming, *A History of Anglican Liturgy* (2nd edn, London: Macmillan, 1982), p. 179. See further on Hamon L'Estrange, p. 18.

11 Sparrow is not mentioned by Kenneth Stevenson in his excellent study of the Eucharist in the seventeenth century, *Covenant of Grace Renewed* (1994).

12 Ibid., p. 280.

13 "Thus the true sacrifice is offered in every act which is designed to unite us to God in a holy fellowship, every act, that is, which is directed to that final Good which makes possible our true felicity.... For sacrifice is a 'divine matter', in the phrase of the old Latin authors, even if it is performed or offered by man." Augustine, *The City of God*, tr. Henry Bettenson (Harmondsworth: Penguin, 1972), p. 379.

14 "I beseech you therefore, brethren, by the mercies of God, that ye present your bodies a living sacrifice, holy, acceptable unto God, which is your reasonable service." (KJV).

15 Newman noted one or two "historical inaccuracies" in Sparrow's work such as the ascription of the *Te Deum* to St Ambrose and the Athanasian Creed to St Athanasius, but, Newman admits, they "are not of consequence enough to require more than this passing allusion". Editor's Preface to Sparrow's *Rationale* (Oxford: John Henry Parker, 1839), p. x.

2

Hamon L'Estrange, *The Alliance of Divine Offices* (1659)

Hamon L'Estrange (1605–60) was born in 1605, the second year of the reign of James 1, in Hunstanton, Norfolk. His father was Sir Hamon L'Estrange (1583–1654) and his family could trace its Hunstanton connection back to the twelfth century.[1] L'Estrange was educated at Eton and Christ's College, Cambridge, and he entered Lincoln's Inn in 1626 but was never called to the bar. Being a person of means, he preferred to devote himself to theological study, in his own words, "in the vales of rural recess". He remained a devout layman, and during the Civil War he was a staunch royalist, serving as a colonel in the king's army. His first published work was entitled *God's Sabbath* (1641), defending the sabbath as a holy and divine institution.

L'Estrange's fortune and estate in Norfolk was sequestered in 1649 and remained under sequestration until 1652. But in adversity his major energies were taken up by his debates with the cantankerous Peter Heylyn (1599–1662), who was chaplain to Charles 1, and following deprivation of his preferments under the Commonwealth, later Sub-Dean of Westminster after the Restoration.[2] When in 1655 L'Estrange published his conciliatory *Reign of Charles I*, Heylyn roughly dismissed him as "stiffly principled in the Puritan tenets, a semi-presbiterian at the least in form of church government, a nonconformist in matter of ceremony, and a rigid sabbatarian in point of doctrine".[3] The real point at issue was that L'Estrange's royalist credentials were unquestionable and yet at the same time he had been critical of Laudian innovations in ceremonials and their part in bringing about the Civil War. Heylyn himself was a staunch supporter of Archbishop Laud, who had been executed in 1645 during the Civil War period.

L'Estrange's response to Heylyn's attack on him was his best-known work, *The Alliance of Divine Offices* (1659), a learned study of the Anglican BCP from 1549 which deliberately steers a careful course between the Roman Catholic and Puritan positions. The significance and lasting value of L'Estrange's work is indicated by its later inclusion in the Library of Anglo-Catholic Theology in 1846 under the oversight of John Keble, John Henry Newman, William Palmer and other leaders of the Oxford Movement. Its full title is magnificently extensive—and significant:

The
Alliance of Divine Offices
Exhibiting all the Liturgies
Of the
Church of England
Since the Reformation;
As also
The Late Scotch Service-Book,[4] with all Their
Respective Variations;
And upon them all
Annotations,
Vindicating the Book of Common Prayer from all the main objections
Of its adversaries, explicating many parcels thereof hitherto
Not clearly understood, shewing the conformity it beareth
With the Primitive Practice, and giving a fair prospect into
The Usages of the Ancient Church.
To These is added at the end,
The Order of Communion set forth 2 Edw. VI.

The third edition of 1699 adds even more:[5]

The Form of Ordination, &.
Additions and Alterations made in the Liturgy, &.
Prayers in the Convocation.
Form of Prayer used in King Charles the Second's

16   THE BOOK OF COMMON PRAYER AND ITS COMMENTATORS

Chapel at the Hague.

Prayers in the Time of an Invasion.

Prayers at the healing.

The title page concludes with a significant Latin quotation from Tertullian:

Quod apud multos unum invenitur, non est erratum, sed traditum.

Long before he wrote *The Alliance of Divine Offices*, L'Estrange had been involved in debates which involved Charles I himself, as well as the marquess of Worcester,[6] as to the differences between Protestantism and Catholicism. From the start he presented himself as a defender of Protestantism, addressing himself to Lady Anne L'Estrange of Hunstanton in these words as one

> who dare tell Rome to her teeth, that that thing which she calls her Religion is but meer policy, not founded upon Christ or his Apostles, but new modell'd in most, and those the weightiest Points, within these last five hundred years.[7]

On the other hand, L'Estrange also took up the defence of the BCP and the Church of England and its bishops against "Smectymnuus" and "his" defence of the Presbyterian form of Christian ministry in a publication of March 1641.[8]

Between these extremes of Presbyterianism and Roman Catholicism, L'Estrange wrote his defence of the Prayer Book and its liturgy with countless references back to Richard Hooker and other Anglican divines. The work of a genuine scholar, at once devout and well read, *The Alliance of Divine Offices* seeks to establish the continuity of the Prayer Book (at least in its 1549 form) with its medieval predecessors. Of Holy Communion, L'Estrange clearly acknowledges that "our service hath its original from the Mass-book". More importantly for L'Estrange, the Church of England "has her resort to the ancient fathers, to their godly orders she conforms herself, leaving the Romanists to the yesterday devised innovations of their Church".[9] L'Estrange's primary concern is to show clearly the apostolic and patristic roots of the Book of Common Prayer, indicating its primitive antiquity as opposed to what he regards as the relatively recent liturgical developments of the Roman Church. The Church of England alone was truly catholic and apostolic. Indeed, the "most noble parts" of the English liturgy, he asserts, were "extant in the usage of the primitive Church long before the popish mass was ever dreamt of".[10]

If L'Estrange focuses most insistently on the patristic sources of the BCP, referring to them with a considerable degree of critical discernment, he is also clearly familiar with many of the most significant medieval liturgical authorities, with frequent references to the writings of Alcuin of York (c.740–804), Bishop William Durandus of Mende, Bishop William Lyndwood (c.1375–1446)[11] and others. L'Estrange also shows an extensive and detailed knowledge of medieval liturgical uses, in particular the Sarum Rite and the English Primers. The *Alliance* was the first work on the Prayer Book to make a comparison of the Books of 1549, 1552 and 1559 (with the 1637 Scottish Liturgy) in parallel columns—a pattern to be followed by others in the nineteenth century such as William Maskell[12] and William Keeling in *Liturgiae Britannicae* (1842). L'Estrange also shows an extensive knowledge of contemporary scholarship in defence of the BCP, citing most often two scholars whose work was also recovered by the Oxford Movement and Tractarians in the nineteenth century—Herbert Thorndike (1598–1672) and his work *Of Religious Assemblies and the Public Service of God* (1642),[13] written to defend the apostolicity of the episcopal government of the Church as opposed to the Presbyterians, and Bishop Anthony Sparrow and his *Rationale*.

As a layman, L'Estrange almost entirely lacks the pastoral concerns and sensitivity of Bishop Sparrow. But he is a far more careful, and indeed learned scholar. Thus, for example, while Sparrow seems content to remain with the Athanasian authorship of the creed which bears his name,[14] L'Estrange offers a learned and detailed note arguing that such a tradition "is fabulous". There is no reference to the so-called Athanasian Creed, writes L'Estrange, in "Nazianzen, Basil, Chrysostom, nor any other of the primitive fathers" and indeed little evidence of it until some thousand years after Christ. Archbishop Ussher (1581–1656), "that great enquirer into ancient rarities", cites a reference to King Aethelstan about the year 924 where "it is called *Fides Sancti Athanasii*, 'The Creed of St Athanasius'". L'Estrange concludes that the Athanasian Creed, though certainly not by Athanasius, is at least as old as the age of Gregory, giving "satisfaction it is enough that it is ancient" and therefore worthy of inclusion in the English Prayer Book.[15]

L'Estrange's commentary on Holy Communion[16] is detailed and carefully annotated to demonstrate that

> the whole action of the sacred Communion is elemented of nothing but sacrifices and oblations. So in our Church, so in the Apostolic, which should be the grand exemplar to all; and though our Church varieth somewhat in the mode, from the first original, yet in the substance her practice is conformable.[17]

He is clear that in Holy Communion there should be a commemoration of the dead, citing the dyptics mentioned in the Fifth General Council of Constantinople (553),[18] that the "consecration" of the elements of bread and wine is not simply by the recital of the words "Take, eat, this is my body" etc.—but by the whole action of blessing and thanksgiving,[19] and that an epiclesis, or invocation of the Holy Spirit, is evident in the liturgies of St Basil and St Chrysostom.[20] In short, L'Estrange's theology of the Eucharist is remarkable for its "catholic" insights and arguments that were hardly so developed again until the middle years of the nineteenth century.[21]

L'Estrange was clear that his purpose in writing *The Alliance of Divine Offices* was properly to educate the Church and its clergy in Anglican theology and liturgy as preserved in the Prayer Book of the Church of England. As in every age of the Church —our own included—he was aware that the clergy of the Restoration Church did not always get things right in their theology and they needed proper instruction. He writes:

> Far be it from me to charge the generality of our new ministry with these blemishes: Confess I must and will, many, very many of them, are excellently qualified and endowed with gifts proper for this sacred duty, and do exercise those gifts to the great

edification of their congregations; but in the mean time, if such miscarriages have actually happened already, or may so hereafter, through the violent passions of other men misprincipled, may it not justly be judged a matter of scandal and offence, to such as have a due value for that holy ordinance, and consequently may not those worthier men be conceived guilty of the crime, through whose misprovidence these errors have come to pass?[22]

People of the church should set aside their differences, suggests L'Estrange, and (like Sparrow) join in the use of "set forms" of worship and prayer as prescribed in the authorized Prayer Book. Until such agreement be reached amongst church parties, and a proper, learned and apostolic form of public worship be followed, L'Estrange concludes, "slender hopes have I to see much of either order or edification in the service of our Church".[23] These weary words seem sadly familiar today.

Notes

[1] In more recent times, in the early twentieth century, P. G. Wodehouse was a friend of the now named Le Strange family, and a frequent visitor to Hunstanton Hall.

[2] Heylyn's other major opponent was the church historian Thomas Fuller (1608–61). Both Fuller and L'Estrange were publicly critical of Archbishop Laud and his role in provoking the Civil War.

[3] Quoted in the ODNB article by W. A. Shaw (revised Sean Kelsey). For more on this debate see Anthony Milton, *Laudian and Royalist Polemic in Seventeenth-Century England: The Career and Writings of Peter Heylyn* (Manchester: Manchester University Press, 2007), pp. 174–5.

[4] The Scottish Prayer Book of 1637.

[5] There was a second edition, published posthumously in 1690.

[6] The marquess of Worcester, otherwise known as Lord Herbert of Raglan, was immensely wealthy and a stalwart royalist who had been brought up as a Roman Catholic. Charged with high treason in 1653, he was released in the following year and devoted himself to his passion for engineering and inventions, including one which was a prototype of the steam engine. See his

Century of Inventions (1655).

[7]   Quoted in ODNB.

[8]   "Smectymnuus" was in fact the initials of the five authors of the book—Stephen Marshall, Edmund Calamy, Thomas Young, Matthew Newcomen and William Spurstow.

[9]   Hamon L'Estrange, *The Alliance of Divine Offices* (4th edn, Oxford: John Henry Parker, 1846), p. 38.

[10] Ibid., p. xi.

[11] Lyndwood's *Provinciale*, in five books, is the greatest work on English canon law from the later Middle Ages. The *Provinciale* was reprinted in 1679.

[12] See Chapter 12.

[13] L'Estrange is not averse to criticism of the liturgy of the Prayer Book where it appears to diverge from ancient use. For example he writes, citing Thorndike's *Of Religious Assemblies*: "Though all our liturgies stand silent in it, yet may I not omit what here by the way doth offer itself as observable, viz. that at the close of the Eucharistical prayer, the ancient manner was for the people to contribute the Amen; which the annotator, Mr. Thorndike, and some other learned men, conceive to be the mind of St. Paul, 1 Cor. xiv.16." *The Alliance*, p. 318.

[14] See also p. 13, Note 15 on Newman's gentle correction of Sparrow.

[15] L'Estrange, *The Alliance of Divine Offices*, pp. 143–4.

[16] Ibid., pp. 224–331.

[17] Ibid., pp. 270–1.

[18] L'Estrange cites the authority of "Vicecomes and other ritualists". William Palmer, in *Origines Liturgicae*, 4th edn (London: Francis & John Rivington, 1845), Vol. 1, p. 132, is highly dismissive of "Joseph Vicecomes, doctor of theology at Milan", when he attempts to trace the Ambrosian liturgy back to the apostolic age.

[19] L'Estrange, *The Alliance of Divine Offices*, p. 315. In this, L'Estrange is remarkably prophetic of the arguments of Walter Howard Frere and Gregory Dix in the twentieth century.

[20] Ibid., p. 317.

[21] See, for example, Alf Härdelin, *The Tractarian Understanding of the Eucharist* (Uppsala: Uppsala University, 1865).

[22] L'Estrange, *The Alliance of Divine Offices*, pp. 52–3.

[23] Ibid., p. 53.

3

Thomas Comber, *A Companion to the Temple* (1672–98)

Thomas Comber's extensive writings have not survived well in the pages of modern scholarship and readership. Horton Davies, in his magisterial work *Worship and Theology in England* (Vol. 2, 1975), has described Comber's work as "prolix, thorough, accurate, and deadly dull, except when he forgot to be devotional and turned controversial".[1] C. J. Stranks in his study entitled *Anglican Devotion* (1961) describes Comber's *Companion* as "laborious and diffuse".[2] Such criticism, though it has its point, is not entirely fair, and a little later Davies admits that a work like Comber's vast multi-volume work *A Companion to the Temple* (1672–98)[3] did much to foster "an informed appreciation of the Prayer Book, cultivated loyalty to the Church of England, and promoted liturgical devotion".[4]

Thomas Comber was born in Westerham, Kent in 1645, of relatively modest parentage, and as a child suffered a great deal from poor health. His early education was largely under the care of the Revd Thomas Walter in his local school at Westerham, which prepared Comber for entry to Sidney Sussex College, Cambridge in 1659. He maintained himself as an undergraduate through a number of charitable grants, and he left the University in 1663 with only his BA degree to show for his student years. But in the same year, aged 18 and well below the legal canonical age for ordination, he was ordained deacon, quickly moving to Stonegrave in the North Riding of Yorkshire as curate. Ordained priest in 1664, Comber became linked to a number of the leading families in North Yorkshire, marrying Alice Thornton in 1668 (despite opposition from her family)

22   THE BOOK OF COMMON PRAYER AND ITS COMMENTATORS

and succeeding in the following year to the crown living of Stonegrave near Helmsley in North Yorkshire.[5]

It was at this time that Comber embarked on his energetic writing career, publishing the first volume of his devotional commentary on the Book of Common Prayer (and here specifically on the Daily Office), *A Companion to the Temple and the Closet*, in 1672. This original title of the work is significant, for its purpose was to link the public worship of the Church with private devotion through the use of the Prayer Book. Together with *A Companion to the Altar* (1675) on holy communion, baptism and confirmation, two further volumes of *A Companion to the Temple* appeared in 1679, resulting in Comber being presented at court in May 1679 after Princess Anne used his work in preparation for her first communion.[6] From thereon he moved in high places and at court.

Holding two livings near York in plurality, Comber was made a prebendary of York Minster in 1677, becoming its precentor in 1683. Through the offices of Archbishop Sancroft, Comber was awarded the degree of Doctor of Divinity in 1678. Though a staunch royalist, Comber deeply opposed James II's promotion of Roman Catholicism and, despite his long-held regard for Charles I and Charles II and his loathing of Protestant dissent, on the accession to the throne of William and Mary in 1689 he readily accepted the new settlement, becoming chaplain-in-ordinary to William and Mary in 1692.[7] In 1691, he became Dean of Durham after his friend, the former Dean Granville, became a Nonjuror.[8] Comber remained in Durham until his death in November 1699.

There is much about Comber as a priest which we may criticize. He was a pluralist who clearly neglected the care of his parishes while he remained a hugely ambitious man forever seeking preferment in the Church, a trait perhaps stemming from his humble origins. Furthermore, and like many in his age, he was quite capable of trimming his ecclesiastical sails to suit the current political wind. Yet his major work, *A Companion to the Temple*, together with *A Companion to the Altar*, remained for a long time an important contribution to Prayer Book studies, being reprinted in full in the middle of the nineteenth century. Following upon the example of such earlier works as Anthony Sparrow's *Rationale* of 1655, Comber's vast commentary combines extensive, if not very original, learning (which Charles Wheatly was later to draw directly upon) with a devotional intent that draws together the Prayer Book as used both in public worship and private prayer and reflection. Indeed, Comber's work is not only a guide to devotion, but it might be said that the very reading of it is itself a devotional act, though one requiring considerable patience.[9]

Comber, like so many others, was concerned to promote a primitive and scriptural vindication of the Prayer Book, based upon the work of his immediate predecessors like Sparrow and L'Estrange. Like them, too, he draws upon more recent Anglican authorities of the sixteenth and seventeenth centuries, not least, of course, Book V of Richard Hooker's *Of the Laws of Ecclesiastical Polity* (1593). In his Preface to *A Companion to the Temple*, Comber directs his words to three kinds of reader whom he names as—"mistaken dissenters", the "ignorant", and "devout servants of God" (that is, as far as he is concerned, practising Anglicans), all of whom are to be taught and, in their various ways, encouraged.[10] Working methodically through the BCP in order, Comber draws extensively on the Prayer Book's deep roots in Scripture as well as describing an impressive, if entirely conventional, array of patristic sources from Justin Martyr and Tertullian to St John Chrysostom, St Ambrose, the Sacramentary of St Gregory and St Augustine of Hippo. He was also, like Bishop Jeremy Taylor and others in the seventeenth century, keen to root the Prayer Book in the classical literature and culture of ancient Greece and Rome. But, in addition, he makes extensive use of medieval sources and liturgies from the Sarum Rite to Durandus' *Rationale* and the writings of St Bernard. References to more recent scholarship include the work of Martin Bucer and Jacques Goar[11] as well as Hooker, Henry Hammond[12] and William Cave.[13]

Comber's method of working through the prayers of the liturgy is systematic and threefold—and, it has to be admitted, often extremely verbose. He begins by demonstrating the structure of a prayer or exhortation, before, secondly, offering a discourse on its meaning and significance. Finally, each prayer is printed in the context of an often lengthy explanatory expansion and paraphrase for devotional use, with the words of the original prayer embedded in it in capital letters. To give a brief example, here is the Prayer Book's first benediction at the end of the prayers for the visitation of the sick, followed by Comber's expansion and paraphrase.

Book of Common Prayer:

> O Saviour of the world, who by thy Cross and precious Blood hast redeemed us, Save us, and help us, we humbly beseech thee, O Lord.

Comber's paraphrase:

> Holy Jesus, through whose merits and intercession all our comforts are obtained, O SAVIOUR OF THE WORLD, who hast mercy sufficient for all mankind, and WHO BY THY cruel death upon the CROSS, by the torments of thy body, and the spilling of thy dear AND PRECIOUS BLOOD, as a sacrifice to thy Father's justice, HAST REDEEMED US from the vengeance due unto our sins; do thou, who hast done all this for us, SAVE US from everlasting damnation, AND HELP US to escape the dreadful wrath of God, WE HUMBLY BESEECH THEE, O LORD, for death will not be terrible to us, when thou hast taken away its sting, and reconciled us to our heavenly Father.[14]

The language of sacrifice is clearly indicative of Comber's Anglican High Church theology, and it can be imagined that such paraphrases of longer prayers can be extremely extensive, often running to as much as 40 pages for one prayer! But his method has a very clear end: that to use the Prayer Book with heartfelt devotion requires patient and intelligent understanding of its theology and history. He believes, quite rightly, that proper devotion is intelligent devotion. As Comber puts it, with typical prolixity, in his Preface to the first volume of his work, speaking of the words of the liturgy:

> When once we have thoroughly pondered them and made our souls fully acquainted with these pertinent and comprehensive expressions of our constant necessities, we shall find our hearts actuated with holy enlargements, and powerfully attracted into the prosecution of the requests made by our lips; and our minds would have no other employment in these duties, but to annex

the sense to the words, and its most vigorous affections to that sense, which is true devotion.[15]

Theologically and in their forms of spirituality, Comber's writings reflect a broadly Laudian sensibility within the tradition of the Book of Common Prayer. He writes not infrequently of "our royal martyr, king Charles the First" and is drawn, in true Laudian manner, to a powerful sense of the beauty of holiness in the words of the Anglican liturgy rather than showing any particular concern for the details of ceremonial and rubric. Comber's primary concern is with the words of devotion and worship. In some ways, despite his own seeming carelessness as a parish priest, Comber is most at home in taking his reader in a pastoral manner through the prayers of the occasional offices—the wedding service, the visitation of the sick, the burial service and prayers and the "churching" of women. His tone is consistently pastoral, even sympathetic, while maintaining the context of the ancient and apostolic traditions that underlie the Prayer Book. Thus, in his extensive writing on the Order for the Visitation of the Sick, having established the antiquity of the tradition of pastoral care for the sick in the Epistle of James (5:14–15), St Polycarp and Tertullian,[16] Comber details at length the Church's responsibilities to those who are ill and possible preparation for death. In his pastoral concerns, far from being deadly dull, Comber's writing can at times provide an echo to the far better known and deeply loved works of Bishop Jeremy Taylor on *Holy Living* (1650) and *Holy Dying* (1651) together with Taylor's "Prayers containing the Whole Duty of a Christian, and the Parts of Devotion fitted to all Occasions and furnished for all Necessities".[17]

In the context of the restoration of the monarchy after 1660, with its recovery of the Prayer Book to a central place in the life of the Church of England, Comber wrote in his 1678 Dedicatory Epistle of his final volume on the occasional offices, to William Sancroft, Archbishop of Canterbury:

> The end proposed to myself in all this hath been, to vindicate the Church of England, and restore these her offices to their due esteem; as also to direct the consciences, to resolve the scruples,

and to assist the devotion of all such as may be concerned in the use of any of them.[18]

Owing, perhaps, to their prolixity, Comber's works during the Restoration period and after never attained the popularity of Sparrow's *Rationale* or the anonymously published and widely read *Whole Duty of Man* (1658), a devotional manual on the Christian life with 17 discourses, one to be read each Sunday, three times each year.[19] Nevertheless, his writings were frequently reprinted and then recovered in the nineteenth century, and thus Thomas Comber played his part in the scholarly placement of the Book of Common Prayer as at the heart of the public and private liturgical and devotional life of the Church of England, a living text indeed to be read, marked, learnt and inwardly digested.[20]

In some ways, one of the best modern "commentaries" on Comber's *Companion to the Temple* is a book which never mentions Comber once, indeed, being primarily concerned with a slightly earlier period of English Protestantism—Alec Ryrie's *Being Protestant in Reformation Britain* (2013). For Ryrie, like Comber, bases his work on two assertions:

1. "Christianity is an incorrigibly intellectual religion."
2. Converts to Christian doctrines "still have lives to live". In the pause, possibly of many years, between the birth of faith and the death of the body, there may be "decades which the Christian has somehow to fill and through which he or she must keep, and grow in, the faith".[21]

Ryrie in his book describes this Christian life in terms of emotions, prayer and intelligent engagement with the "word" in the Bible and Prayer Book, and in the passage through life. Comber offers, and sets out to explain, the true guide through such a life—to be found in the words, sacraments and offices of the Book of Common Prayer.

Notes

[1] Horton Davies, *Worship and Theology in England, Vol. 2: From Andrewes to Baxter and Fox, 1603–1690* (Princeton: Princeton University Press, 1975), p. 117.

[2] C. J. Stranks, *Anglican Devotion: Studies in the Spiritual Life of the Church of England between the Reformation and the Oxford Movement* (London: SCM Press, 1961), p. 156.

[3] *A Companion to the Temple* was reprinted in seven large volumes by Oxford University Press in 1841.

[4] Davies, *Worship and Theology, Vol. 2*, p. 117. The only modern edition of Comber's work are his "autobiographies and letters", edited in two volumes by C. E. Whiting in 1946–7.

[5] Notable for its Anglo-Saxon and Norman parish church, Stonegrave currently has a population of just over 100.

[6] In 1682, Comber became a chaplain to Princess (later Queen) Anne.

[7] C. E. Whiting describes Comber as a whig in his later days post-1688, though his previous royalist attachments seem to have been unwaveringly tory. Whiting (ed.), *The Autobiographies and Letters of Thomas Comber*, 2 vols, Surtees Society (1946–7), Vol. 2, p. xii.

[8] Nonjurors refused to take the Oath of Allegiance to William and Mary after 1688 on the grounds that to do so would be to break their previous oaths made to James II and his successors. Among the Nonjurors, there were nine bishops and some 400 clergy.

[9] See further, Benjamin Crosby, "Read, Mark, Learn and Inwardly Digest: The Prayer Book and Private Devotion in Prayer Book Commentaries from Sparrow to Mant", *Journal of Anglican Studies* 21 (2023), pp. 87–105 (93–5).

[10] See further, Rémy Bethmont, "Promoting Anglican Liturgical Spirituality: Thomas Comber's *Companions* to the Book of Common Prayer", *Revue Française de Civilisation Britannique* XXII:1 (2017), pp. 1–12,(3).

[11] Jacques Goar (1601–54), was a French Dominican and liturgist.

[12] Henry Hammond (1605–60) was an Anglican priest and staunch loyalist under Charles I. His *Practical Catechism* (published anonymously in 1645) was very popular. He was also a pioneer in biblical criticism.

[13] William Cave (1637–1713) was an Anglican divine, canon of Windsor and chaplain to Charles II. His reputation as an historian is largely owing to his

28 THE BOOK OF COMMON PRAYER AND ITS COMMENTATORS

work *Primitive Christianity: or, The Religion of the Ancient Christians in the First Ages of the Gospel* (1675).

[14] Thomas Comber, *A Companion to the Temple: or, A Help to Devotion in the Use of the Common Prayer*, Vol. IV, "Of the Occasional Offices" (Oxford: Oxford University Press, 1841), p. 331.

[15] Quoted in Rémy Bethmont, "Promoting Anglican Liturgical Spirituality", p. 4.

[16] Comber, *A Companion to the Temple*, Vol. IV, p. 186.

[17] Bishop Jeremy Taylor's works were frequently reprinted through the nineteenth century and up to the present time.

[18] Comber, *A Companion to the Temple*, Vol. IV, p. 5.

[19] The consensus of scholarly opinion is that the author of this work was Richard Allestree (1621/22–81), a royalist clergyman and later Provost of Eton College from 1665. There are, however, some 30 other possible authors who have been suggested! See further, Stranks, *Anglican Devotion*, pp. 123–48.

[20] See the collect for the Second Sunday in Advent in the Book of Common Prayer.

[21] Alec Ryrie, *Being a Protestant in Reformation Britain* (Oxford: Oxford University Press, 2013), p. 1.

4

The contributions of the Antiquarians to the history of the Book of Common Prayer and its commentators: Joseph Bingham, *Origines Ecclesiasticae, or The Antiquities of the Christian Church* (1708–22); David Wilkins, *Concilia Magnae Britanniae et Hiberniae* (1737)

Rosemary Hill begins her book on antiquarianism, the sometimes obsessive collecting of ancient texts and artifacts, *Time's Witness* (2021), with a comment on the nature of "history" which is illuminating for the important and persistent claim, as much theological and ecclesiological as historical, that the Anglican Book of Common Prayer is indeed "catholic and apostolic":

> High probability is certainly one reason for accepting a particular historical account, but it is only one. What follows here, I suggest, demonstrates that the history we have, at any given moment, is the history we want.[1]

It might seem strange to find the names of Joseph Bingham (*bap*.1668–1723) and David Wilkins (1685–1745) amongst Anglican commentators on the Book of Common Prayer. Although they were both ordained Anglican clergymen, they did not write specifically upon the BCP, but are remembered for their tireless labours respectively in antiquarian investigations and collections in the early history of Christianity and in the history of British Church councils from 446 to 1717. It seems strange, that is, until one remembers the insistent concern of Prayer Book commentators from the earlier seventeenth century and before to establish the continuity of worship in the English Church from apostolic times, through the early Church and the liturgies of the medieval period until the time of the Prayer Book itself—promoting the belief that the Church of England was in continuity with the universal Church since the very earliest Christian times, the English Reformation merely an occasion for the correction of the detours of medieval "Popish" errors in a continuous and living tradition of worship from the time of Christ until the present.

Antiquarians like Bingham and Wilkins in the early eighteenth century were essentially largely uncritical accumulators of the "facts" and the material remains of history. They were not so much historians as antiquarians, a term that has come to be regarded rather negatively after the eighteenth century, although one recent book by Rosemary Hill, *Time's Witness*, has done a great deal to recover its true and legitimate value. And indeed throughout the works of numerous Anglican liturgists, pastoralists and Prayer Book commentators in the nineteenth century, the names of Bingham, Wilkins, Richard Gough (1735–1809) and others appear repeatedly. The modern editor of John Henry Newman's *Sermons of 1824–43*, Placid Murray, writes at the outset of his commentary of Newman's "considerable dependence on Joseph Bingham's *Origines Ecclesiasticae*".[2] Nor was Newman alone in this. The reason for this dependence is that Bingham's antiquarian labours in the field of early Christianity nourished and substantiated that vision of the Church with which we are now so familiar—that of the continuity of the Church of England from the time of Christ until the present, sustained in its liturgy and worship, and this meant, for Anglicans through hundreds of years, in the Book of Common Prayer.

This vision can be seen, in some ways, as a romantic one, though none the less important for that, and the term is perhaps not to be dismissed too readily. It was not an accident that Newman and the leaders of the Oxford Movement in the early nineteenth century looked back to the

Romantic poets and writers for inspiration. In his *Apologia Pro Vita Sua* (1864), Newman mentions first Sir Walter Scott, then moves on to Samuel Taylor Coleridge, to Robert Southey and to William Wordsworth as early sources of inspiration, and as writers who acted on their readers by "stimulating their mental thirst, feeding their hopes, setting before them visions, which once seen, are not easily forgotten".[3] Rather like the Romanticism which fed a vision for the nineteenth-century Church of England in both the words of the liturgy and the stone of English Gothic churches, the antiquarians of the eighteenth century provided a mass of historical materials to nourish a living tradition of liturgical continuity, a longing for an "unattainable ideal"[4] that was yet sustained in public worship drawn from the Prayer Book—that the Church of England was ancient and apostolic, and was catholic in its worship.

The Revd Joseph Bingham did not enjoy much success in his lifetime, either as a scholar or as a clergyman. Throughout his life, he struggled to maintain his large family on a small stipend. To some extent, he had only himself to blame. After a successful undergraduate career at University College, Oxford, he embarked upon a promising life as a fellow of his college, until a somewhat intemperate sermon preached in October 1695 on the subject of the Trinity led him to be denounced as heretical and an Arian. He resigned his college fellowship and began his lifelong struggle with poverty and failure to secure preferment from his modest living of Headbourne Worthy near Winchester. Certainly his character did not help him. He was, it seems, habitually argumentative and his writing betrays a man embittered by failure and, as he saw it, ill use in the Church. But through it all he laboured valiantly and produced his remarkable *Origines Ecclesiasticae*, published in ten volumes over a period of 14 years. Bingham stated his aim as being:

> to give such a methodical account of the antiquities of the christian church as others have done of the Greek and Roman and Jewish antiquities, by reducing the ancient customs, usages, and practices of the church under certain proper heads, whereby the reader may take a view at once of any particular usage or custom of christians for four or five centuries.[5]

Origines is a remarkable achievement, and this massive work continued to be read and reprinted well into the nineteenth century. My own copy was published in 1834, over 100 years after it was first published, printed here not in ten but in eight volumes, revised and edited by Bingham's grandson Richard Bingham, who was also a clergyman and a canon of Chichester Cathedral. Richard enjoyed the posthumous success of his grandfather's labours and did rather better for himself in the Church. Working from original patristic sources, *Origines* provided a mine of material to be employed in countless works of Anglican liturgy and commentaries on the BCP to support the vision of the continuity of worship through its carefully reconstructed and researched description of the early Church, its theology and liturgy.

Let us take an illustrative example of the volumes of *Origines*, from Volume 7 in Richard Bingham's nineteenth-century edition. The volume begins with the author's dedication to his current diocesan bishop, Charles Trimnell, Bishop of Winchester.[6] Here Bingham makes it clear that his purpose was to serve the Church of England, educating those of other Protestant denominations who had drifted away to bring about "a nearer union to the Church of England".[7] Bingham's lengthy Preface, originally written for Volumes 9 and 10 of the first edition, is little more than a rant against a certain "A. Blackamore", who in 1722, it seems, produced a two-volume work entitled *Ecclesiae Primitivae Notitia*—a summary of Christian antiquities. Bingham takes up the story in his Author's Preface:

> I confess I was very much surprised at first with the title and epistle dedicatory, thinking it to be some new work, that had done some mighty thing, either in correcting my mistakes, or supplying my deficiencies, after twenty years hard labour in compiling my *Origines* for the use of the Church. But as soon as I looked into the Preface, and a little into the Book itself, I found it to be only a Transcript of some part of my *Origines*, under the notion of an Epitome, though no such thing is said in the Title Page. This seems to be an art of the gentleman, and the ten booksellers that are in combination with him, to render my

JOSEPH BINGHAM AND DAVID WILKINS 33

books unuseful and his own more valuable, as containing all that
I have said and something more at a less price.[8]

It is a familiar story of plagiarism, and Bingham employs some 50 pages
of his Preface to dismantle in great detail the book of his detractor. It
was, perhaps, a labour wasted, for when Bingham begins his proper
task in earnest his writing becomes clear, and his learning, though of its
time, is prodigious. Briefly to summarize Volume VII, Bingham begins
with a review from biblical times of the great festivals of the Church,
starting with Sunday. He then proceeds with the festivals of Christmas
(Christ's Nativity), Epiphany, Easter (the Paschal Festival), Pentecost (or
Whitsuntide) and the festivals of apostles and martyrs. Finally there is a
long dissertation on the history of Lent.

Bingham's chapter on the festival of Easter is typical of his scholarship.
His prose is surprisingly readable, as he takes us through the meaning
of the term *pascha*, the theology of Easter and evidence of the liturgy of
Easter in the early Church. He is a careful reader of ancient sources up
to Eusebius and beyond, his style descriptive rather than argumentative.
He takes his narrative up to St John Chrysostom and St Gregory of Nyssa
in the late fourth century. It is a mine of generally reliable information
on early Church liturgical practice.

A very different form of historical and theological resource for the
historian of the English liturgy was the work of David Wilkins, the author
(although editor would be a more correct term, and the title page does not
bear his name) of the *Concilia Magnae Britanniae et Hiberniae* (1737) in
four volumes. This is a vast collection of documents and letters relating
to British Church councils and religious affairs from 446 to 1717. Wilkins
was born in Lithuania of Prussian parents, his original name being Wilke,
which he anglicized as Wilkins. Of his early education little is known,
but by 1707 we find him studying in the Bodleian Library, Oxford, with
a wide, if somewhat inaccurate, knowledge of numerous ancient and
Semitic languages. Reception of his early work was decidedly mixed so
that though Oxford refused to bestow an MA on him in 1712, only five
years later Cambridge awarded him a Doctorate of Divinity. After he
became an Anglican clergyman, Wilkins was made Librarian at Lambeth
Palace in 1715, contributing much to the cataloguing of its manuscript

34   THE BOOK OF COMMON PRAYER AND ITS COMMENTATORS

collection, though accumulating detractors along the way. The politician Sir Edward Harley described him as "a very great scoundrel", while Thomas Hearne, the Librarian of the Bodleian, called him "a vain ambitious man, of little judgement, tho' great industry".[9] Despite such detractions, Wilkins flourished, and as an Anglican clergyman he gained some preferment, becoming a canon of Canterbury in 1721 and Archdeacon of Suffolk in 1724. Marriage to the daughter of Lord Fairfax of Leeds Castle, Kent was accompanied by a handsome dowry. He did well for himself.

Yet despite this somewhat rackety life and admittedly careless scholarship, John Wilkins earned himself a place in our narrative focused on the BCP. The ODNB sums up his work in these words: "He was primarily a copyist and a compiler, often lacking thoroughness and discrimination." And his achievements as a copyist and compiler in his *Concilia Magnae Britanniae* were considerable. It is a work on a vast scale and here I will look briefly at the fourth volume, which covers documents from the Church councils from 1546 to 1717, during which period the Prayer Book came into being and reached its final form in 1662. The documents are in both English and Latin, and they are printed without commentary though they are meticulously indexed. The first two are from the *Synodus provincialis Cantuar* and the *Synodus provincialis Eboracensis*, the first (Canterbury) being the text of "a proclamation for the abolishing of English books after the death of Ann Askew, set forth by the king" (July 1546), and the second, "injunctions given by the most excellent prince Edward the Sixth . . . to all and singular his loving subjects, as well of the clergy as of the laity".[10] Following the documents in sequence provides dramatic and first-hand insight into the development of Anglican liturgy and the Prayer Book in the sixteenth and seventeenth centuries.

For example, one of the first documents printed in full is the royal Proclamation of Edward VI and text of the English "Order of the Communion" of 1547.[11] The introduction reads:

> For so much as in our high court of parliament, lately holden at Westminster, it was by us, with the consent of the lords spiritual and temporal, and commons there assembled, most godly and agreeably to Christ's holy institution, enacted that the most

blessed sacrament of the body and blood of our Saviour Christ, should from henceforth be commonly delivered and ministered unto all persons within our realm of England and Ireland, and other dominions under both kinds, that is to say, of bread and wine (except necessity otherwise require) lest any man fancying and deviling[12] a sundry way by himself, in the use of this most blessed sacrament of unity, there might arise any unseemly and ungodly diversity.[13]

There follows a full text of the "Order of Communion", anticipating the Prayer Book of 1549. Edward issues his Proclamation and liturgical text by the advice of his "most dear uncle the duke of Somerset, governor of our person, and protector of all our realms".

Moving on to 1550, and citing as his source Peter Heylyn's *History of the Reformation* (*Ecclesia restaurata*) of 1661, Wilkins prints the order from council to Bishop Ridley[14] to replace altars with communion tables. Ridley is commanded, in order "to maintain the common quiet of our realm", to strip away altars in the diocese of London, and "instead of them a table to be set up in some convenient part of the chancel, within every such church or chapel, to serve for the ministration of the blessed communion".[15] It should be noted that the term "altar" is used in the 1549 Communion, replaced in 1552 with "the Lord's Table".[16]

Finally, Wilkins draws upon the extensive papers of Bishop Thomas Tanner (1674–1735), himself a noted antiquarian and writer,[17] to print an extended account of the Savoy Conference of 1661, convened in the reign of Charles II to review the BCP. The document contains a detailed list of participants, bishops, Presbyterian divines and assessors, gathered "to advise upon, and review the said book of Common Prayer, comparing the same with the most ancient liturgies, which have been used in the church in the primitive and purest times".[18] The account of the Conference's inconclusive termination is recounted briefly in the agreed report to the king:

That the church's welfare, that unity and peace, and his majesty's satisfaction were ends, upon which they were all agreed; but as to the means, they could not come to any harmony.[19]

The work of antiquarians like Bingham and Wilkins, though not always accurate, provided fertile resources for the commentators on the Book of Common Prayer who are the primary subjects of this book, providing the historical detail to illustrate the vision of liturgical continuity dating back to the "primitive and purest times" of the Church, through the Middle Ages and the first hundred years of the Prayer Book from 1549 until the settlement of 1662. The Church of England as catholic and apostolic was, in some respects, a romantic vision, though an important one that persisted over the centuries and for good reason. Ecclesiological in its nature, it was close to what Rosemary Hill has described as "a re-conception of history as a continuum in which generations do not simply replace one another in a forward march of improvement, but form links in a chain".[20] For the Church of England after the Reformation, the anchor for such a chain was the Book of Common Prayer.

As scholarship developed in the nineteenth century, not least liturgical scholarship, as we shall see in the work of Palmer, Maskell and others, so the writings of antiquarians like Bingham and Wilkins did not always fare well, though their works continued to be widely employed and cited. Among them we might also have mentioned the work of Richard Gough (1735–1809) and the second volume of his *Anecdotes of British Topography* (1768, new edition, 1780), which offers considerable detail on the uses, books and medieval liturgical practices of Sarum (Salisbury).[21] A later scholar of medieval liturgy, the rather testy William Maskell, whom we shall meet in more detail later,[22] was utterly dismissive of Gough's carelessness, complaining of his most "egregious blunders".[23] It is often the habit of scholars of a later age to criticize the errors or naivety of their predecessors. But such men as Bingham, Wilkins, Gough and even the rather dilettante Thomas Frognall Dibdin (1776–1847) and his somewhat fanciful *Bibliographical Decameron, or, Ten Days Pleasant Discourse upon Illuminated Manuscripts* (1817) played their part in the history of commentaries upon the Book of Common Prayer since 1549 and its place in the longer history of the English Church before the middle of the sixteenth century.

Notes

1   Rosemary Hill, *Time's Witness: History in an Age of Romanticism* (London: Allen Lane, 2021), p. 9.

2   Placid Murray OSB (ed.), *John Henry Newman, Sermons, 1824–1842*, Vol. 1 (Oxford: Clarendon Press, 1991), p. xv.

3   J. H. Newman, *Apologia Pro Vita Sua* (1864), ed. Ian Ker (Harmondsworth: Penguin, 1994), p. 99. It might be remembered also that Scott was an antiquarian before he was a novelist, the title of his third novel being *The Antiquary* (1816).

4   Hill, *Time's Witness*, p. 4.

5   Joseph Bingham, quoted in the ODNB.

6   Charles Trimnell (1663–1723) was Bishop of Winchester from 1721 to his death in 1723. Bingham repeatedly sought a canonry at Winchester, "where", he once wrote, "my business chiefly lies among the books of the library".

7   Joseph Bingham, *Origines Ecclesiasticae: or, the Antiquities of the Christian Church*, Vol. VII, ed. and rev. Richard Bingham (London: William Straker, 1834), p. iv.

8   Ibid., pp. vii–viii.

9   Quoted in the ODNB.

10   David Wilkins, *Concilia Magnae Britanniae et Hiberniae*, Vol. 4 (London, 1737), pp. 1–8.

11   Edward VI was crowned on 20 February 1547. No precise date is given for the 1547 Proclamation.

12   Wilkins is not always an accurate copyist. Might "deviling" be "devising"?

13   Wilkins, *Concilia Magnae*, Vol. 4, p. 11.

14   Nicholas Ridley (*c.*1500–55), Bishop of London.

15   Wilkins, *Concilia Magnae*, Vol. 4, p. 65.

16   For a fuller note see Brian Cummings (ed.), *The Book of Common Prayer: The Texts of 1549, 1559, and 1662* (Oxford: Oxford University Press, 2011), p. 697.

17   Bishop Tanner's most notable work is *Notitia Monasticae* (1695), a history of the religious houses in England and Wales.

18   Wilkins, *Concilia Magnae*, Vol. 4, p. 571.

19   Ibid., p. 572.

20   Hill, *Time's Witness*, p. 3.

[21] See further, Matthew Cheung Salisbury, "Rethinking the Uses of Sarum and York: A Historiographical Essay", in Helen Gittos and Sarah Hamilton (eds), *Understanding Medieval Liturgy* (London: Routledge, 2016), pp. 105–6.

[22] See Chapter 12.

[23] William Maskell, *Monumenta Ritualia Ecclesiae Anglicanae* (2nd edn, Oxford: Clarendon Press, 1882), Vol. 1, pp. ix–x. Maskell goes on to lambast another antiquarian (or perhaps more accurately bibliographer), Thomas Frognall Dibdin, and his *Bibliographical Decameron* (1817), in which Dibdin frequently simply copies Gough (and his mistakes).

5

Charles Wheatly, *A Rational Illustration of the Book of Common Prayer* (1710)

As we move into the eighteenth century, and away from the more tumultuous religious and political changes and debates of the seventeenth, the tradition of Prayer Book commentary, both scholarly and devotional, becomes more established and widely used, though essentially in continuity with the work of L'Estrange, Sparrow, Comber and others. For example, Robert Nelson (1656–1715) was a layman who became for a while a Nonjuror after 1691. He returned to the established Church in 1710, though retaining his Jacobite sympathies. His book *Companion for the Festivals and Fasts of the Church of England* (1704)[1] was widely read and reprinted as late as 1875.[2] Nelson also wrote a widely read devotional work on the Eucharist entitled *The Great Duty of Frequenting the Christian Sacrifice* (1706).

But undoubtedly the outstanding and most widely read Prayer Book commentary of the early eighteenth century was the learned and sometimes cantankerous *The Church of England Man's Companion, or, A Rational Illustration of the Harmony, Excellency, and Usefulness of the Book of Common Prayer* (1710) by Charles Wheatly, which became the standard work for more than a century and profoundly influenced the Oxford University of the earlier part of the nineteenth century in the work of Bishop Charles Lloyd, William Palmer and the later Tractarians. It continued to be printed as late as 1890. My own copy has the signature of Edward C. Ratcliff (1896–1967), the distinguished Cambridge liturgist and regius professor of divinity, on the inner cover. By his many markings on the text, Ratcliff clearly read Wheatly attentively.[3]

Charles Wheatly was born in London in 1686 and was educated at Merchant Taylors' School and St John's College, Oxford.[4] Elected a fellow of his college in 1707, he graduated with his BA in 1710 (MA in 1713). For much of his life, Wheatly was a country clergyman, holding the combined benefices of Brent and Furneux Pelham in Hertfordshire from 1726. An active controversialist in the Church, he defended the use of the Nicene and Athanasian Creeds within orthodox belief and opposed the spread of Methodism. But his primary work for which he is remembered was the *Rational Illustration of the Book of Common Prayer*, as it became known, which went through countless editions in the eighteenth and nineteenth centuries, and six in his lifetime alone. It was substantially annotated by G. E. Corrie (1793–1885), the Master of Jesus College, Cambridge and Norrisian Professor of Divinity in Cambridge University, for the edition published in 1858 for Cambridge University Press.[5] Wheatly was rector of Brent and Furneux Pelham, Hertfordshire for 16 years. He died there in 1742.

In his writing on the Prayer Book, Wheatly worked substantially and openly with the scholarship of the previous century, emphasizing once again the "primitive" origins of the BCP which continued through the Middle Ages. On the title page of his book, we find the following admission of his work:

> The whole being the substance of every thing material in Bishop Sparrow, Mr. L'Estrange, Dr. Comber, Dr. Nicholls, and all other former ritualists, commentators, or others, upon the same subject.[6]

He was perfectly well aware of the succession in which he was writing. But already in Wheatly's liturgical work there is a new and different tone from that of his seventeenth-century predecessors—less engaged with the devotional life of the Church, less political and more strictly "academic". With Wheatly, the proper understanding of the Prayer Book had become a matter for the rectory study and the library. Given the wide popularity of his book, Wheatly was writing, it seems, for a new age and a new readership after the upheavals of the seventeenth century, a readership, perhaps, less political and more confined to the clergyman's study and to the libraries of the churches and cathedrals of the Church of England. (The original title, *The Church of England Man's Companion*, however, was omitted in later editions.)

Wheatly begins his work with a defence of the "lawfulness and necessity of a national precomposed liturgy",[7] and this he sets out to establish in a clear series of carefully argued steps. From the Jewish and patristic origins of the BCP he moves on to a brief history of worship in England before the Reformation with a reference to "the present Roman Breviary and Missal",[8] together with the changes brought about under Henry VIII. The tone is dry, informative and historical, moving systematically from 1549 up to 1662. His arguments are not new or in any way original, stressing liturgical continuity rather than change during the English Reformation. He makes the point that

> it was not the design of our Reformers, nor indeed ought it to have been, to introduce a new form of worship into the Church, but to correct and amend the old one; and to purge it from those gross corruptions which had gradually crept into it; and so to render the divine service more agreeable to the Scriptures, and to the doctrine and practice of the primitive Church in the best and purest ages of Christianity.[9]

The argument reflects back to the previous century in the Church of England and forward to the Prayer Book theology of the Oxford Movement and the *Tracts for the Times* in the next century. Looking back to some words of Thomas Comber, Wheatly identifies and itemizes the particular virtues of the Anglican Prayer Book which are, he suggests, as follows:

1. It is comprehensive, exact and inoffensive.
2. The wisest may exercise their knowledge, and the ignorant may pray with understanding.
3. Nothing is omitted.
4. It comprises most things we would pray for in private.
5. It is short so as not to tire true devotion.
6. Its doctrine is pure and primitive.

7. Its ceremonies are few and innocent.
8. Its language is significant and perspicuous.
9. Its words and phrases are scriptural or expressions of the first and best ages.

In short, the Prayer Book is comprehensive and economical, offering pure doctrine and the basis for proper devotion.

The more scholarly and clerical tone of Wheatly's *Rational Illustration* is suggested first by his frequent reference to John Johnson's legal handbook for clergy, *The Clergy-Man's Vade Mecum: Or, An Account of the Antient and Present Church of England; The Duties and Rights of the Clergy; and of their Privileges and Hardships* (1706).[10] There are also many more references to the medieval liturgy of the English Church than appeared in commentaries of the previous century. Notable, too, is an etymological and philological concern for the language of the BCP, anticipating the later interests of the clergymen scholars of the nineteenth century. Wheatly clearly intended his book to be read and used by the parochial clergy drawing upon the three great pillars of the Church of England—reason, Scripture and antiquity.[11] Thus he carefully articulates the Anglican doctrine of the Eucharist and the "real presence", to be distinguished from the "entirely different" doctrine of transubstantiation and in which the words "real and essential" are clearly to be understood apart from "corporal presence".[12]

Wheatly sustains throughout his work a constant note of antipathy towards Roman Catholicism (to be distinguished from the Catholic Church of which the Church of England is clearly a part), linking it at every opportunity with his disapproval of Presbyterianism. For example, of the observance of Sunday as a day of celebration he writes:

> It having never been the practice of the Catholic Church, not indeed of any part of it, except the Roman, and that which has too many marks of its parent, the Presbyterian Church in Scotland, to allow of humiliation or fasting on Sundays, which are appointed for duties of a different nature.[13]

In his discussion of the Calendar, Wheatly allows himself a detailed account of "Romish Saints'-days", while dismissing the majority as they are, he writes, frequently found to be "feigned and fabulous", or else retained merely for cultural reasons "for the sake of such tradesmen, handicraftsmen, and others, as are wont to celebrate the memory of their tutelar Saints".[14] There is in much of his provision of such information for his reader, a tone of somewhat superior weariness as he continues in his account of "Romish Saint's-days" that are retained in the Calendar of the BCP:[15]

> But [I] must first bespeak my reader not to think that I endeavour to impose all these stories upon him as truths; but to remember that I have already given him warning that a great part of the account will be feigned and fabulous. And therefore I presume he will excuse my burdening him with testimonies; since though I could bring testimonies for everything I say, yet I cannot promise that they will be convincing. But however, I promise to invent nothing of my own, nor to set down anything but what some other of the blind Romanists superstitiously believe.[16]

Wheatly is not one to mince his words.

In his extensive commentary on Holy Communion (pp. 290–381), Wheatly is clear throughout in his preference for the 1549 Prayer Book, commenting that the reordering of the Prayer of Oblation in 1552 leaves it "mangled and displaced".[17] He begins his commentary by making a clear distinction between Holy Communion and Morning Prayer, which are "designed to be used at a different time" and not, as was generally the case in the eighteenth century, run together as, effectively, one long and extended service on a Sunday morning.[18] Furthermore he advocates the regular celebration of Holy Communion which in the "purest ages of the Church" had been daily, though now "the shameful neglect of religion with us has made the imitation of this example to be rather wished for than expected".[19] In very brief space, he refers to the ancient Eucharistic liturgies of the Church, necessarily composed, since "it does not appear that our Saviour prescribed any particular method" himself.[20] From the liturgies of St Basil, St Chrysostom, St Ambrose and St Gregory, these in turn drawing upon the ancient liturgies of Jerusalem, Alexandria and Rome—"none of these being received as of divine origin"—the "excellent compilers of our Common Prayer" produced the liturgy of 1549, following the example of patristic practice, though they

> no otherwise confined themselves to the Liturgies that were before them, than out of them all to extract an Office for themselves: and which indeed they performed with so exact a judgment and happy success, that it is hard to determine whether they more endeavoured the advancement of devotion, or the imitation of pure antiquity.[21]

For Wheatly, the true Anglican Eucharistic liturgy was to be found in the 1549 Prayer Book and the culprit for the damage done in 1552 was Martin Bucer, from whose amendments as regius professor of divinity at Cambridge until his death in 1551, "this momentous and principal Office of our Liturgy had the misfortune to suffer very great alterations".[22]

Wheatly anticipates the presiding culture of the eighteenth century in his often dry logic and appeal to reason. For him there are no depths of trickery to which the "Romish Church" cannot stoop. Given their doctrine of transubstantiation,

> In the Romish Church indeed they always stand before the altar during the time of consecration;[23] in order to prevent the people from being eyewitnesses of their operation in working their pretended miracle.[24]

The Church of England, of course, "pretends no such miracle" in its service of Holy Communion.

Thus we perceive that Wheatly's tone can be waspish, at the very least, and breathes a fire of anti-ecumenism which he inherited from the controversies of the previous century and which persisted in the Church of England more or less throughout the following century, as we shall see. Nor was his scholarship original, though it was thorough, and so his *Rational Illustration* remained a standard work in Anglican liturgical writing for well over 100 years, profoundly influencing the

Oxford Movement through the 1823 lectures of Bishop Charles Lloyd, and from him the writings of William Palmer.[25]

Notes

[1] Geoffrey Cuming misprints this title as *Companion for the Festivals and Feasts of the Church of England*. See *A History of Anglican Liturgy* (2nd edn, London: Macmillan, 1982), p. 131.

[2] By SPCK, of whom Nelson was a notable supporter.

[3] Edward C. Ratcliff was the author of *The Book of Common Prayer: Its Making and Revisions* (1949).

[4] His mother was a descendant of Sir Thomas White, the founder of St John's College, Oxford in 1555.

[5] Apart from his university responsibilities, Corrie was also a devoted parish priest in Newton-in-the-Isle, Ely.

[6] William Nicholls (1664–1712), canon of Chichester Cathedral, was the author of the *Comment on the Book of Common Prayer, and Administration of the Sacraments* (1710). See further, Chapter 6.

[7] Charles Wheatly, *A Rational Illustration of the Book of Common Prayer*. With additional notes by G. E. Corrie (Cambridge: Cambridge University Press, 1858), p. 1.

[8] Ibid., p. 17.

[9] Ibid., p. 17.

[10] John Johnson (1662–1725) was a clergyman in the Laudian tradition. For many years vicar of Cranbrook in Kent, he was known as "Johnson of Cranbrook". Most of his books were anonymous, and they include a paraphrase of the *Book of Psalms*, working from the Coverdale translation in the BCP.

[11] See William Marshall, *Scripture, Tradition and Reason: A Selective View of Anglican Theology through the Centuries* (Dublin: The Columba Press, 2010).

[12] Wheatly, *A Rational Illustration*, pp. 380–1.

[13] Ibid., p. 617.

[14] Ibid., p. 42.

[15] For example, for January: Lucian, Hilary of Poitiers, Prisca, Fabian, Agnes and Vincent.

[16] Wheatly, *A Rational Illustration*, p. 43.

[17] Ibid., p. 350. Compare, more recently, W. H. Frere in *Some Principles of Liturgical Reform* (1911) and the "growing number of clergy and others who are barely able to be satisfied with the jejuneness of our Consecration Prayer" (p. 193). He is referring to the 1662 Prayer Book, which follows the order of 1552. More recent Anglican liturgical revisions have addressed this problem of the ordering of the Eucharistic prayer.

[18] See further on Morning Prayer and Holy Communion, Bishop Richard Mant, Chapter 8, pp 64–5.

[19] Ibid., p. 290.

[20] Ibid., p. 291. In a footnote to the 1858 edition, Corrie refers the reader to the first volume of William Palmer's *Origines Liturgicae* for a full account of the "Liturgies of Antiquity", and to William Maskell's *Ancient Liturgy of the Church of England* for their medieval descendants.

[21] Ibid., p, 291.

[22] Ibid., p. 291.

[23] Westward facing. Wheatly's preference for the position of the priest is at the north end, as was the custom into the nineteenth century (and occasionally beyond). See, for example, T. F. Simmons, "The North Side of the Lord's Table" (*Contemporary Review*, October 1866), discussed in David Jasper and Jeremy Smith, *Reinventing Medieval Liturgy in Victorian England: Thomas Frederick Simmons and The Lay Folks' Mass Book* (Woodbridge: The Boydell Press, 2023), p. 20.

[24] Wheatly, *A Rational Illustration*, p. 353.

[25] See Chapters 9 and 10.

6

William Nicholls, *A Comment on the Book of Common Prayer and the Administration of the Sacraments* (1710)

In the same year that Charles Wheatly published his *Rational Illustration of the Book of Common Prayer*—1710—Dr William Nicholls (1664–1712) published his lengthy and wordy *Comment on the Book of Common Prayer*, a book of over 700 pages, dedicated to Queen Anne. The *Comment* consisted largely of the text of the Prayer Book with vast footnotes and *apparatus criticus* that far outweighed the original in size. It was a work that should be set somewhere between those of Comber and Wheatly, being deeply learned (to the point of pedantry) and yet at the same time it was designed for private devotional use in the Church, based upon the offices and liturgy of the BCP.

William Nicholls was born in Donnington, Buckinghamshire and educated at St Paul's School, London. He matriculated at Magdalen Hall, Oxford in 1680, but moved to Wadham College, graduating in 1683. After ordination in 1688, he served in a number of parochial positions before becoming a canon of Chichester Cathedral in 1707. However, most of his life was spent in literary labours in London, often in some poverty, culminating in his great *Comment on the Book of Common Prayer* of 1710, a work which probably cost him his health and almost certainly contributed to his death in 1712. Learning—and perhaps devotion—comes at a price.

Apart from his *Comment*, for which he is best known, Nicholls was a prolific writer, his works including a *Short History of Socinianism* (1691), and most significantly his Latin treatise *Defensio Ecclesiae Anglicanae* (1707–8), which he subsequently also translated into English as *A Defence*

47

48 THE BOOK OF COMMON PRAYER AND ITS COMMENTATORS

of the Doctrine and Discipline of the Church of England, published posthumously in 1715. This attracted considerable attention amongst foreign as well as English churchmen and scholars. More important from our perspective here were his paraphrases of the Psalms, published in 1708 and intended to encourage the devotional life of laypeople in the Church as well as his fellow clergy.

Nicholls was a man of immense learning, and his *Comment* was intended for scholars, clergy and lay worshippers in the Church of England. As well as detailed notes on the ancient and patristic origins of the Prayer Book offices and liturgy, he provides a full commentary on the Elizabethan Act of Uniformity, which prefaces the book, and, perhaps most importantly, further paraphrases of prayers and creeds, rather after the manner of Thomas Comber, to assist the understanding of the Anglican laypersons in their devotions. Of these paraphrases, C. J. Stranks in his book *Anglican Devotion* (1961) has written:

> Very often they read into the text more than is to be found there, they use two words for one wherever possible, and spin the thought out to great length, but in spite of this they often furnish a genuine elucidation of the meaning. The Athanasian Creed particularly becomes a much more understandable document for most people in Nicholls' paraphrase. Those in the Morning and Evening Prayer he intended for use as private devotions.[1]

Nicholls' High Churchmanship is ever present—in his evident devotion to the Caroline divines, the works of Bishop Lancelot Andrewes and Bishop John Cosin, and his dismissal of what he calls the "new fangl'd liturgy" of the Puritan divine Richard Baxter (1615–91), which is "warranted by no Ancient Forms".[2] He is referring to the "Reformed Liturgy" which Baxter wrote to replace the Prayer Book.

Nicholls' title page in 1710 is extraordinary even by the standards of the seventeenth century. It reads as follows:

WILLIAM NICHOLLS

A

Comment on

The Book of Common Prayer and Administration of the Sacraments, etc.

Together with the

Psalter or Psalms of David

Being

A Paraphrase on the Sunday and Holiday-Services, Epistles and Gospels throughout the Year: with NOTES on all the Rubricks, giving an account of all the festivals and Saints-Days observed in the Church; as also the Lives of the Saints, and Days of Distinction mention'd in the Calendar; of the Compilers and Reviewers of our Common-Prayer; of the ancient use of liturgies, of Lessons, Psalmody, Calendars, etc. Of the Defects of the Roman Breviary and Missals, of Horary Times, Sundays, Holidays; of Paschal Cycles, Synagogues, Churches, Chancels, Bells, Church-Musick, Vestments; of Synaxes[3] and Rites observed in the Communion; of Baptismal Rites, of Catechists and Catechumens; with the method of Catechizing, in a Full exposition of the Catechism of the Church of England; Confirmation, Sponsers, and Vicarious Interrogatories; of Matrimonial Contracts, Paranymphs, Impediments, etc. Of Prayers for the Sick, and other ancient usages concerning Clinicks; of Absolutions, Penances, Sepulture, etc. With a PARAPHRASE of the whole Book of Psalms, according to the Common-Prayer-Book translation.

The Text of the whole being compared and Amended according to the Sealed Books;[4] and the Psalms compared with the Translation of the Great Bible.[5]
At the end of the Book are subjoined the Additional
Notes of Bishop Andrews, Bishop Cosin, etc.

Nicholls is nothing if not ambitious and thorough. His High Churchmanship is clear, but he is ever the pastoral realist. He recommends individual confession and absolution, yet grants freedom to the individual. Confession and Absolution are:

> things very convenient to be put into practice, when Persons
> cannot quiet their own consciences otherwise; but still leaves
> them at their Liberty whether they will make use of this means
> or no.[6]

With the spiritual life of the worshipper ever in mind, Nicholls begins his Preface in the *Comment* with an emphasis on the purpose of his paraphrase of the Prayer Book daily offices as being to encourage personal devotion for lay people as well as clerics. At the same time, his scholarly concern to establish the ancient and universal roots of the BCP is clear in his extensive writings on patristic sources and his review in the Preface of the Prayer Book's pre-Reformation foundations, beginning in the English medieval tradition with St Osmond [sic] of Salisbury (*c*.1080) as the origin of the Sarum rite.[7] Nicholls concludes his history of the BCP with references to the *King's Primer* of 1545, Cranmer's Litany of 1544[8] and a discussion of the influence of Jean Calvin and Martin Bucer on the Prayer Book revisions of 1552.

Not satisfied with the more than 700 pages of the *Comment*, Nicholls went on to publish a *Supplement to the Commentary on the Book of Common Prayer* in 1711. This somewhat bizarre work, also containing an extremely lengthy title page, includes, among discussions of the history of the orders of ministry together with the "mischiefs in several ages accruing from the Papal Supremacy", some strange and indeed unexpected discourses on "the original and progress of navigation, ships of war, and sea-fights". More significantly, Nicholls shows his royalist inclinations in

> A Short History of the Powder Plot; and a Dissertation shewing, that resistance, deposition and murder of Princes, took their first rise from the Pope and his dependents, contrary to Scripture and the constant doctrine of Christian writers for near twelve centuries. Of the Civil War, the King's murder and the Restoration, with some short memoirs concerning the present reign.[9]

Nicholls was a complex, driven character, his life especially in its later stages haunted by poverty. He set his commentary on the Prayer Book, with all its considerable learning and pastoral concerns, in the context of a broad set of historical and cultural concerns. The worship and spiritual life of the Church, for him, was the very heart of all life and society. In his words of dedication to Queen Anne, he seems sure of the success of his work, which was, indeed, like the work of Comber, widely used amongst clergy and the more intellectual layfolk of the Church. He wrote in that dedication:

> I have found, to my great satisfaction; a fresh instance of the Extraordinary Regards, which are still paid to our Liturgy; by seeing in the success of this Commentary which I have published upon it, what, I think, has never happened in the Publishing any Book before; That all the Copies of it are either bought up or bespoken, before it has seen the Light.

His book, he claims, was a sell-out in terms of its subscribers. In spite of this, Nicholls' work can hardly have been seen as easy reading or particularly convenient to use. The *Rational Illustration* of Charles Wheatly, published in the same year as Nicholls' *Comment*, is much shorter and more accessible, but at the same time drier and without Nicholls' pastoral and devotional concerns. Despite his dislike of the "mischiefs" of the Papacy and Rome, Nicholls did, however, publish a translation and adaptation of St Francis de Sales' *Introduction to the Devout Life*, "With a Discourse of the Rise and Progress of Spiritual Books in the Romish Church" in 1701. His works continued to be printed well into the nineteenth century, exemplifying the combination of scholarly learning and devotional attention that accompanied the study and use of the BCP for many centuries.

Notes

[1] C. J. Stranks, *Anglican Devotion: Studies in the Spiritual Life of the Church of England between the Reformation and the Oxford Movement* (London: SCM Press, 1961), p. 160.

[2] William Nicholls, *A Comment on the Book of Common Prayer and Administration of the Sacraments* (London, 1710), p. ix. Richard Baxter played a prominent role in the Savoy Conference of 1661.

[3] Celebrations of the Eucharist.

[4] The Sealed Books were the copies of the 1662 Book of Common Prayer certified with the signatures of the six Commissioners and the great seal

52 THE BOOK OF COMMON PRAYER AND ITS COMMENTATORS

of England, dated 13 December 1662, intended to settle any disputes as to variant wording.

[5] The Great Bible was largely the work of Giles Coverdale and was the translation which Thomas Cromwell ordered to be placed in every parish church in September 1538.

[6] Nicholls, *Comment*, note on the first exhortation in the Communion Service. Sadly the pages after the Preface in his *Comment* are not numbered.

[7] St Osmund (*d*.1099), Bishop of Salisbury, was almost certainly not the originator of the Sarum Use, which probably dates from the early thirteenth century and Bishop Richard Poore (1197/8–1228).

[8] Nicholls dates the Litany as 1549. *Comment*, Preface, p. v.

[9] William Nicholls, *A Supplement to the Commentary on the Book of Common Prayer*, (1711), title page.

7

Thomas Wilson, *A Short and Plain Instruction for the Better Understanding of the Lord's Supper* (1734)

Bishop Thomas Wilson (1663–1755) is included in this series of brief sketches not because he wrote a commentary on the BCP; nor was he a great scholar or particularly concerned to establish the catholic and apostolic credentials of the Prayer Book. Yet his voice is important in the narrative of these short chapters, placing the Book of Common Prayer and its Eucharistic theology at the very heart of the pastoral life of the Church of England in the middle years of the eighteenth century.

Thomas Wilson of Sodor and Man was a thoroughly Prayer Book bishop, looking back to the High Church Anglican tradition of Bishop Lancelot Andrewes and Bishop Jeremy Taylor, and now perhaps best remembered (outside the Isle of Man, which was his see) for his *Short and Plain Instruction for the Better Understanding of the Lord's Supper* (1734). It was a work that lived up to its title, being short and plain but also wise, and it continued to be reprinted well into the nineteenth century and was translated into Manx (1757), French (1817) and Welsh (1846). Wilson was also an important figure, both liturgically and pastorally, for the Oxford Movement: excerpts from his personal *Sacra Privata*, first published posthumously in 1781, and other works, formed material for no less than 12 of the *Tracts for the Times*, where attention was given particularly to his "Meditations on his Sacred Office". Wilson's writings also formed an important element in the Library of Anglo-Catholic Theology, John Keble undertaking to superintend the publication of a complete edition, and Keble also writing a two-volume *Life of the Right Reverend Father in God, Thomas Wilson DD* (1863). Of this, Keble's biographer, J. T. Coleridge, wrote that "it is a storehouse of facts, faithfully recorded, in which is contained all that can be known of an Apostolic Bishop".[1] An Oxford edition of Wilson's *Sacra Privata* was introduced by John Henry Newman. At the conclusion of his *Life*, Keble compared Bishop Wilson with St Augustine of Hippo, and amongst eighteenth-century Anglican divines placed him second in significance only to Bishop Butler:

> If veneration for the Universal Church and unreserved faith in the Bible do yet in any degree prevail in our popular theology,— to him [Thomas Wilson], perhaps, more than to any single divine of later days, with the single exception of his great contemporary Bishop Butler, are these good effects owing.[2]

Thomas Wilson was born in Burton in Cheshire in December 1663, having family connections through his uncle with the Earl of Derby, who also carried the title Lord of Man. These connections were to shape his future life as a bishop. Educated at Trinity College, Dublin, the young Thomas Wilson at first seemed destined for a career in medicine, but instead he was ordained deacon in the cathedral church of Kildare in 1686. Following various curacies and posts in England, including in 1682 serving as domestic chaplain to William George Richard Stanley, Lord of Man and the ninth Earl of Derby, in 1697 Wilson was consecrated Bishop of Sodor and Man,[3] where he remained until his death in 1755. He refused an offer of preferment to the larger and much wealthier diocese of Exeter. It is not difficult to understand the attraction of Thomas Wilson for Newman, Keble and the leaders of the Oxford Movement. He combined a deep personal piety with pastoral energy and attention to both the theological and liturgical life of the Church. Beloved by both the clergy and people of Man, Wilson exercised a strict but benign authority over the spiritual and practical welfare of the people of his diocese. He rebuilt crumbling churches and rectories, established parochial libraries through the vision of his friend Dr Thomas Bray,[4] and promoted the farming life of the community, among other things planting orchards and "several thousand forest trees",[5] when he restored the dilapidated house known as Bishop's Court.

Wilson was also interested in foreign missions and an early supporter of the Society for Promoting Christian Knowledge (SPCK)[6] and he was remarkable in his day for his ecumenism which, as we have seen, was not a notable trait of the eighteenth-century Church of England. Yet the non-conformist hymnwriter Isaac Watts (1674–1748) was an appreciative reader of Wilson's *A Short and Plain Instruction*.[7] Far more extraordinary were his close links with Count Nicolaus Zinzendorf and the Moravian church, which in 1749 offered Wilson the position of "Honorary President of the Reformed Section in the Moravian Church", more oddly designated "Antistes of the Reformed Tropus in the Unity of the Brethren". The bishop, though by then 85 years old, accepted the honour "because he was desirous of doing everything for the Brethren that lay in his power".[8]

The leaders of the Oxford Movement, almost a century after Bishop Wilson's death, were also drawn by his long-running dispute with the tenth Earl of Derby and governor of the Isle of Man, James Stanley, regarding the jurisdiction of the diocesan ecclesiastical courts which Wilson sought to strengthen to improve the discipline of his clergy. The result was a reduction in the revenues of secular disciplinary actions taken by the earl and a two-year legal struggle during which Bishop Wilson was imprisoned for some weeks in miserable conditions in Castle Rushen on Man. His successful appeal to the king and privy council was an important ruling in the High Church struggle against Erastianism and in favour of the Church's freedom to govern itself, which was to flower in the nineteenth century under the principles of the Oxford Movement and after John Keble's Assize Sermon of 1833.

Among Wilson's many writings, by far the most enduring and popular was his *Short and Plain Instruction*, a natural successor to his earlier and much shorter book entitled *Principles and Duties of Christianity in English and Manx* (1707). The full title of the later book reads:

A Short and Plain Instruction
For the Better Understanding of
The Lord's Supper;
With
The Necessary Preparation Required;
For the Benefit of Young Communicants,
And of such as have not well considered this Holy Ordinance:
To which is annexed,
The Office of the Holy Communion,
With proper Helps and Directions for joining in every part thereof
With Understanding and Profit.

Written in simple and straightforward prose that is still readable today, this little work for lay people attending Holy Communion according to the use in the Book of Common Prayer has its pastoral, devotional and theological roots in such works as the late medieval poem that became known as the *Lay Folks' Mass Book*, edited by Thomas Frederick Simmons in 1879.[9] It is essentially a devotional guide, with the text of the Prayer Book liturgy with full rubrics printed in a parallel column beside simple prayers and biblical material for the lay person to use. Its principle seems close to the medieval practice of a dual action in the service, in which the words of the liturgy (though now in English, not Latin) are paralleled by prayers, devotions and reflections being pursued by the lay person while the service is being said by the priest.

Bishop Wilson begins his little book with reference to the two sacraments "appointed by Jesus Christ as most especial means of obtaining grace and salvation", that is baptism and the Lord's Supper.[10] After a brief exposition of the fallen state of humankind from Eden, Wilson, in emphatically sacrificial language, speaks of the "Sacrament" of the Holy Communion for us as "what the tree of life would have been unto *Adam* and *Eve* in Paradise".[11] This is an image of the Eucharist, as Kenneth Stevenson has pointed out, that goes back to Bishop Jeremy Taylor and Bishop Lancelot Andrewes.[12] Brief instructional essays on the Eucharist and the theology of salvation are accompanied by prayers so that the unlearned may be enabled to pray with clear understanding—a recurrent theme in this work as it was in the work of Comber, Nicholls and others, as we have seen. Prayer must be intelligent and thoughtful as well as devout.

After proper preparation the reader of *A Short Instruction* is guided through the text and rubrics of the Prayer Book service with, in Wilson's words, "due edification and instruction". The prayers, exhortations and explanations provided are carefully constructed on pneumatological and trinitarian principles, although, as Kenneth Stevenson has pointed out, in later editions after Wilson's death in 1755, the work was subject to abbreviation which amounted to "a kind of theological–liturgical censorship",[13] mostly crucially in the important edition of Wilson's works edited by Clement Cruttwell in 1781. Significantly (and happily) they were restored in the later Library of Anglo-Catholic Theology edition under the supervision of John Keble.[14] Most significantly they include an English version of the epiclesis, or invocation of the Holy Spirit (to be said "secretly"), drawn from the *Apostolic Constitutions*, Book VIII, a work which in the eighteenth century was taken as being of apostolic origin.[15] Wilson advises his reader:

> *Say secretly,*—Send down thy Spirit and blessing upon this means of grace and salvation, which Thou thyself, O Jesus hast ordained.[16]

Wilson's theology, within the Prayer Book tradition of Archbishop Laud and the Caroline divines, clearly emphasizes the sacrificial nature of the sacrament, the presence of Christ in the consecrated elements (carefully though not closely defined), and the efficiency of the reception of Holy Communion for salvation. He encourages regular communion in his diocese, though his *Short and Plain Instruction* is a practical work and also provides for the "spiritual communion" of those who "through any just impediment are hindered from receiving the Lord's Supper . . . from the hands of Christ's own minister".[17] The work concludes with a brief explanation and paraphrase of the Lord's Prayer and the provision of short forms of Morning and Evening Prayer suitable for both families and individuals.

More personal than this small manual for eucharistic devotion according to the BCP, and never written for publication, are the *Sacra*

Privata of Bishop Wilson, known chiefly through the edition in the Library of Anglo-Catholic Theology. Here, too, there are devotions intended to be used during the celebration of the Holy Communion, not as divergence from the Prayer Book but as a kind of counterpoint to the Church's liturgy. Again the authority of the *Apostolic Constitutions* VIII is in evidence and, as Kenneth Stevenson has pointed out, there is a startling prayer to be offered by the priest at the celebration of the Prayer Book Holy Communion service:

> May I atone thee, O God, by offering to thee the pure and unbloody sacrifice, which thou hast ordained by Jesus Christ. Amen.[18]

Though in the spirit of the seventeenth-century Anglican divines, this certainly stretches Reformation[19] sensibilities by its personalism and its use of the terms "atone" and "unbloody"; yet it also remarkably anticipates the sacramental theology of the Oxford Movement some one hundred years after Bishop Wilson's time.

The Anglican Book of Common Prayer is never far from the thought and use of Bishop Thomas Wilson, both in public office and private prayer. Its sacramental and devotional riches are placed in the service and context of a deeply pastoral ministry which was concerned with the welfare (and sometimes the lapses) of the bishop's clergy as well as the moral, spiritual and practical well-being of all his people in a range of issues from the provision of parochial libraries, to the chastising of those guilty of sexual infidelity, and to practical dealing with the matter of land tenure, whereby the bishop made possible for tenant farmers the virtual ownership of their land.[20] Bishop Wilson was a priest and prelate, a man of wide if not notably deep learning, on whom both the universities of Oxford and Cambridge conferred honorary doctorates of divinity in 1707, but, and perhaps more importantly, also genuinely beloved of his clergy and people. Amongst them, he sustained a tradition of Anglican liturgical piety and scholarship that looked back, through the lens of the Prayer Book, to the sixteenth century and Bishop Taylor (1613–67), and forward to the nineteenth century and the fathers of the Oxford Movement.

Almost the entire adult population of the Isle of Man was present at Bishop Wilson's funeral in March 1755. He had been their bishop for more than 50 years.

Notes

[1] Sir J. T. Coleridge, *A Memoir of the Rev. John Keble, M.A.* (2nd edn, Oxford and London: James Parker & Co., 1869), Vol. II, p. 478.

[2] John Keble, *The Life of the Right Reverend Father in God Thomas Wilson DD.* (Oxford: John Henry Parker, 1863), Vol. II, p. 971.

[3] Kenneth Stevenson explains the origins of the curious episcopal title. "From the sixth century to the ninth, the island had Welsh kings, but these were superseded by Vikings, when they settled the Northern Isles with Man. From 1066 until 1266, the Kings of Man claimed authority over the Hebrides, under Norway, hence the archaic name of 'Sodor and Man', i.e., the 'Southern' Isles (southern, that is, from Norway!) with Man itself." "The Eucharistic Theology of Thomas Wilson (1663–1755), Bishop and Pastor", *Studia Liturgica* 26 (1996), pp. 253–63 (253).

[4] Thomas Bray (1656/8–1730), an Anglican clergyman, was, like Wilson, concerned with the early years of the SPCK and Society for the Propagation of the Gospel in Foreign Parts (later USPG). His scheme for establishing parish libraries in both England and America was successful, over 80 parish libraries being established in England in his lifetime.

[5] Hugh Stowell, *The Life of the Right Reverend Thomas Wilson* (London: F. C. & J. Rivington, Longman & Co., 1822), p. 42.

[6] John Keble, *The Life of Thomas Wilson*, p. 589.

[7] Ibid., p. 759.

[8] Bishop Thomas Wilson, quoted in John Keble, *The Life of Thomas Wilson*, p. 945.

[9] Thomas Frederick Simmons (ed.), *The Lay Folks' Mass Book*, EETS OS 71 (London, 1879). See further, pp. 126–38. See also, David Jasper and Jeremy J. Smith, *Reinventing Medieval Liturgy in Victorian England: Thomas Frederick Simmons and the Lay Folks' Mass Book* (Woodbridge: The Boydell Press, 2023).

10 Thomas Wilson, *A Short and Plain Instruction for the Better Understanding of the Lord's Supper* [1734] (new edn, London: SPCK), p. 1. No date is given for this edition, which I have in my library, but it is printed for use during the reign of Queen Victoria, and therefore must be dated after 1837. On baptism and the Lord's Supper, see Articles XXVII and XXVIII in the BCP.

11 Ibid., p. 16.

12 Kenneth Stevenson, *Covenant of Grace Renewed: A Vision of the Eucharist in the Seventeenth Century* (London: Darton, Longman & Todd, 1994), p. 115; Stevenson, "The Eucharistic Theology of Thomas Wilson", p. 258. Compare also the language used to describe the Bible in "The Translators to the Reader", the essay which prefaces the 1611 King James Bible. Holy Scripture is here described as "a fountain of most pure water springing up unto everlasting life".

13 Stevenson, "The Eucharistic Theology of Thomas Wilson", p. 259.

14 See Sir J. T. Coleridge, *A Memoir of the Rev. John Keble, M.A.*, Vol. II, p. 362.

15 The *Apostolic Constitutions* are a collection of ecclesiastical law and probably date from the fourth century of Syrian origin. They were widely read in the seventeenth and eighteenth centuries. William Whiston (1667–1752) wrote in his *Primitive Christianity Revived* (1711), that "these sacred Christian laws or constitutions were delivered at Jerusalem and in Mount Sion, by our Saviour to the eleven apostles there assembled after his resurrection".

16 Wilson, *A Short and Plain Instruction*, p. 111.

17 Ibid., p. 134.

18 Wilson, *Sacra Privata*, quoted in Stevenson, "The Eucharistic Theology of Thomas Wilson", p. 261.

19 Bishop Wilson does take care, however, to describe the Church of England in his book as a "Reformed Church".

20 The 1704 Act of Settlement in the Isle of Man was largely the formulation of Bishop Wilson.

8

Richard Mant, *The Book of Common Prayer and Administration of the Sacraments ... with Notes, Selected and Arranged* (1820)

Richard Mant (1776–1848) was born in Southampton where his father, also Richard Mant, was the headmaster of King Edward's Grammar School. His mother was the daughter of the antiquarian and scholar clergyman whom we have already encountered, Joseph Bingham (1668–1723), author of the widely read *Origines Ecclesiasticae* (1708–22).[1] Mant was educated at Winchester College where the headmaster was Joseph Warton (1722–1800), better known for his editions of classical poets, including Virgil, than his success as a schoolmaster.[2] Later the young Richard Mant wrote verses in memory of Warton and in 1802 edited the *Poetical Works of Thomas Warton*, Joseph's brother and poet laureate. Mant himself was an ardent though distinctly untalented published poet, his works including *The Simpliciad* (1808), parodying the Lakeland poets Wordsworth, Southey and Coleridge. Mant was later a translator of *Ancient Hymns from the Roman Breviary* (1837), and writer of hymns, his best known today being "Bright the vision that delighted/Once the sight of Judah's seer".

Mant entered Trinity College, Oxford in 1793, from which he graduated in 1797, being elected a fellow of Oriel College in the following year, notable enough to be invited to deliver the Bampton Lectures in 1811, his subject being the evangelical character of Anglican preaching in the face of Methodist criticism. He was ordained in 1803 and after a number of parochial appointments he became, in 1813, domestic

61

chaplain to Charles Manners-Sutton, the Archbishop of Canterbury. He later dedicated his annotated *Prayer Book* to Manners-Sutton in 1820, expressing his gratitude for the "considerate condescension and kind but dignified affability" that he had enjoyed as a member of the archbishop's household. In 1820, Mant was consecrated bishop of the somewhat remote diocese of Killaloe and Kilfenora in County Clare, Ireland, being translated three years later to the more congenial, and far more Protestant, Ulster diocese of Down and Connor, to which was added the diocese of Dromore in 1842. One of his predecessors in his diocese was Bishop Jeremy Taylor[3] in the seventeenth century. Mant, it seems, was an energetic and effective diocesan bishop, his annotated editions of both the Bible and the Book of Common Prayer reflecting his pastoral concerns and energy rather than his scholarly originality. Yet he published widely, his best-known work being his *History of the Church of Ireland from the Reformation to the Revolution* (1840). It was at the instigation of Archbishop Manners-Sutton that Mant (with George D'Oyly[4]) undertook the annotation of the Bible in 1814. Like the later annotated *Book of Common Prayer*, Mant's annotated Bible was very largely made up of a compilation of the scholarly work of others, but it was widely used, influencing, among others, a young W. E. Gladstone.

Richard Mant's annotated *Book of Common Prayer* became a much-used and standard text for Anglican clergymen and was frequently reprinted in the nineteenth century. It is a vast work of almost 1,000 pages, comprising the full text of the Book of Common Prayer of 1662 with extensive footnotes and additions "from approved writers of the Church of England". Mant writes almost entirely for the benefit of parochial clergy, giving advice on the proper conduct of public worship. Thus, for example, his note on the Comfortable Words in the order of Holy Communion is drawn from the writings of Bishop Thomas Wilson,[5] giving advice to a clergyman taking the service:

> These most comfortable words should always be read with great deliberation, that the people may have time to reflect upon them; and to apply them every one to the comfort of his soul; and to prevent all unreasonable fears and doubts of God's gracious pardon and acceptance.[6]

Mant's brief Introduction, a mere 12 pages printed in double columns, gives an account of the "original of 'The Book of Common Prayer', and the several alterations that were afterwards made in it". He makes the briefest mention of the pre-Reformation liturgy prior to the *Bishops' Book* of 1537, published under the title "The godly and pious institution of the Christen man",[7] and his description of the medieval uses is, to put it mildly, dismissive. The great rites of Sarum, York and so on were merely, in his terms, "a collection of prayers":

> Before the Reformation the Liturgy was only in Latin, being a collection of prayers made up partly of some ancient forms used in the primitive Church, partly of some others of a later original, accommodated to the superstitions which had by various means crept by degrees into the Church of Rome, and were from thence derived to other Churches in communion with it; like what [sic] we see in the present Roman Breviary and Missal.[8]

It does seem likely, indeed, that Mant had little knowledge of, or indeed interest in, pre-Reformation liturgy. Indeed, it has long been noted that his translations from Latin hymnody in his collection *Ancient Hymns from the Roman Breviary* show little solid knowledge of medieval hymnody or liturgy.[9] And so, dismissing the pre-Reformation Church for its "gross corruptions" he turns to the two Edwardine Prayer Books of 1549 and 1552 in which, he writes, we find "the divine service more agreeable to the Scriptures, and to the doctrine and practice of the primitive Church in the best and purest ages of Christianity".

Mant, though he applauded, admittedly critically, the "good and laudable motives" behind the Oxford Movement's *Tracts for the Times*, clearly held a preference for the Prayer Book of 1552, which, in his view, removed elements of the 1549 book that "savour too much of superstition",[10] and much of this improvement he attributes to the benign influence of Martin Bucer and Peter Martyr. Stewart Brown describes Mant as among the "prominent High Churchmen in the Irish Church" alongside Bishop Jebb and others,[11] yet Mant mentions in particular, and with true evangelical fervour, the removal in 1552 of the use of oil in baptism, the "prayers for souls departed" and the omission of the "invocation of the Holy Ghost" in the consecration of the Eucharist. Recounting briefly the Hampton Court (1604) and Savoy (1661) Conferences, Mant brings his short narrative up to 1662, giving the names of his authorities in italic print at the end of the final paragraph (as he does throughout his work)—Charles Wheatly, William Nicholls and Bishop George Tomline.[12] Mant draws throughout on the work of others, making no claims at all to originality of scholarship. His list of patristic authorities is taken directly from Wheatly's *Rational Illustration of the Book of Common Prayer*,[13] and in particular he draws heavily on Thomas Comber's *Companion to the Temple*, " a work to which the present Editor [of the Prayer Book] is principally indebted for his annotations".[14] Other writers he uses frequently include names now familiar to the present reader—Bishop Sparrow, Hamon L'Estrange, Thomas Wilson, Richard Hooker, Bishop Cosin and Jeremy Taylor.[15]

Mant regards the Book of Common Prayer quite simply as the perfect liturgy, asserting that "there is no part of religion but is in the offices of the Church of England". Throughout his annotated *Book of Common Prayer*, he addresses the working parish clergyman, a readership made even more specific when he published in 1845 his *Explanation of the Rubrics in the Book of Common Prayer, with Special reference to Uniformity in Conducting the Service*. By 1847, this later work had been edited in the United States by an Episcopal priest in New York, W. D. Wilson, with some editing and additional notes particularly relevant to the American Prayer Book of 1789.

Mant's *Explanation of the Rubrics* is essentially two episcopal letters to his clergy in the diocese of Down and Connor, and Dromore, followed by a shorter letter to candidates for ordination. The first letters, printed as one essay, are entitled *Liturgical Discrepancy: Its Extent, Evil, and Remedy*. The shorter essay to ordinands is entitled *Liturgical Harmony: Its Obligation, Means, and Security against Error; whether Popish or Puritanical*.

In the much longer *Liturgical Discrepancy*, Mant moves in detail through the rubrics for the two Sunday morning services of Morning Prayer and Holy Communion, with additional comments on baptism after the second reading in Morning Prayer. He insists that conformity to the Prayer Book is the duty of all clergy, for it is "the Book of Common

Prayer, which the Church has prescribed, and which her ministers have voluntarily and solemnly undertaken, for the guide of their ministrations: the same, without adding or diminishing; that, and no other".[16] The Prayer Book is the instrument for "conveying the Church's intentions" precisely, and thus no prayer is to be publicly used other than that authorized in the BCP. In particular, Mant asserts:

> Extemporaneous prayer in public worship is altogether repudiated by the Church, and she allows no prayers but those of her own liturgy. If, therefore, any prayer be used . . . it should be taken from the Book of Common Prayer.[17]

Any idea of the revision of the Prayer Book, a process which was to preoccupy so much of the nineteenth century, was anathema to Bishop Mant.[18] The worship of the Church, he asserts, tolerates no "innovation", though the Reformation exercised the very different principle of "renovation" in the face of the "medieval inventions" of Rome—and was thus a process of restoration rather than revision, which is completed in the 1662 Prayer Book:

> This was the principle of the Reformation. We had erred from the primitive Church in our religious rites and ceremonies: and so it was the aim and endeavour of our spiritual fathers, the regenerators of our National Church, to bring us back to the observance of God's law in our public worship.[19]

Mant's ideal is the "principle of perpetual Liturgical Conformity".[20]

In his shorter address to those preparing for ordination, Mant focuses on the four essays printed at the beginning of the Prayer Book, all of them printed with the "convocational and parliamentary authority" of the 1662 Prayer Book:

1. The Elizabethan Act of Uniformity
2. The Preface
3. Concerning the Service of the Church
4. Of Ceremonies.

His underlying concern is for "uniformity in public prayers",[21] to overcome the "medieval departure from the primaeval usage of the Church". He dismisses any recent interest in the Church of England with the "Romish Breviary".[22] Thus Mant warns his young ordinands:

> We may trust in God's goodness, that there is little peril of such a corrupt admixture being again introduced by authority into our Church services. Yet aware as we are of the high commendation, which in certain quarters has been of late bestowed on the Romish Breviary in comparison with our Book of Common Prayer; of the excessive veneration testified for the blessed Virgin; of the fondness which has betrayed itself for the devotees of celibacy and monastic institutions, and for the propagators of curious peculiarities in the middle ages; of the propensity to accredit and circulate legendary tales of saints, and to institute new commemorative services in their honour: it may be not altogether an unreasonable suggestion, which should caution you against custom that formerly prevailed, of mixing up for popular instruction human fables and fictions with divine truth.[23]

His prospective clergy are to beware of "objectionable rites" that were becoming evident in the Church of England and Ireland, manifest in public worship in the "reiterated gesticulations" of officiating priests, the use of "sacerdotal vestments", exorcisms and chrisms at baptisms, the worshipping of the reserved sacrament, "creepings to the cross" and "multitudinous bowings and crossings of the person". The list goes on. Clearly Mant was aware that his Church, or at least elements of it, was changing in its manner of worship and in such "new" ways as were not suited to conservative and Protestant Ulster. He concludes his address by returning again to the revisions made in the 1552 Prayer Book and its rubrics.

Shortly after the publication of Mant's letters to his clergy and ordinands in 1844, the Dean of Down in his diocese published a short tract entitled *The Churchman's Duty*. Bishop and Dean joined in their demands that their parish clergy should be firmly led by their "authentic formulary and guide, the Book of Common Prayer".[24] Since the first publication of his annotated *Book of Common Prayer* in 1820, Mant had become the recognized voice of a conservative, broadly evangelical defence of the BCP in the then united Church of England and Ireland at a time when the evangelical movement was powerful in Ireland in its renewal of the spiritual life of the Church and its campaign to convert Roman Catholics.[25] Mant's *Prayer Book* was, in many ways, the culmination of earlier commentaries on the BCP, both scholarly and pastoral, over the past two centuries as we have been following them.[26] His charge to his clergy, delivered on 4 and 5 July 1843, was entitled:

> Rubrickal conformity: the churchman's duty, and as such recognized by our bishops, divines, and ritualists, in the seventeenth and eighteenth centuries.

The years in the nineteenth century after Mant's death would see a change in the connotations of the term "ritualist", though his concern for and close adherence to the rubrics of the Prayer Book would continue in the debates of the newly restored Convocations of Canterbury and York, leading to the *Convocation Prayer Book* of 1880.[27]

Mant remained as bishop of his diocese until his death in Ballymoney, Co. Antrim, on 2 November 1848. His son, Walter Bishop Mant (1808–69) was also ordained and was the Archdeacon of Down from 1828 until his death. His biography of his father, *Memoirs of the Right Reverend Richard Mant, D.D.*, was published in 1857.

Notes

[1] See Chapter 4.

[2] During Warton's time at Winchester, ill discipline resulted in no less than three mutinies by the boys, in one of which Mant was involved.

[3] Jeremy Taylor (1613–67) was appointed Bishop of Down and Connor at the Restoration of the monarchy in 1660, becoming also Bishop of Dromore in 1661.

[4] George D'Oyly (1778–1846) was, like Mant, domestic chaplain to Archbishop Manners-Sutton. A priest of scholarly habits, he was also treasurer to the

68   THE BOOK OF COMMON PRAYER AND ITS COMMENTATORS

Society for Promoting Christian Knowledge (SPCK), which underwrote the cost of the annotated Bible.

[5] See Chapter 7.

[6] Richard Mant, *The Book of Common Prayer and Administration of the Sacraments* (6th edn, London: Francis & John Rivington, 1850), p. 310.

[7] Ibid., p. v.

[8] Ibid., p. v.

[9] See comment in the entry on Mant in John Julian, *A Dictionary of Hymnology* (London: John Murray, 1907), p. 713. Mant's scant knowledge of Latin hymnody is in contrast to the translations of the Tractarian Isaac Williams (1802–65) and even more the slightly later J. M. Neale. See Chapter 14.

[10] Mant, *The Book of Common Prayer*, p. vi.

[11] Stewart J. Brown, "Ireland, Wales, and Scotland", in Stewart J. Brown, Peter B. Nockles and James Pereiro (eds), *The Oxford Handbook of the Oxford Movement* (Oxford: Oxford University Press, 2017), p. 443. Certainly Mant agreed to be a patron of the Cambridge Camden Society, though he resigned from this in the light of charges of "Puseyism". Nigel Yates, *The Religious Condition of Ireland, 1770–1850* (Oxford: Oxford University Press, 2006), pp. 286–7.

[12] Bishop George Pretyman Tomline (1750–1827) was successively Bishop of Lincoln and Winchester. His *Elements of Christian Theology* (1799) was written for candidates for ordination.

[13] Mant, *The Book of Common Prayer*, p. xiv.

[14] Ibid., p. x.

[15] Other texts he uses fairly frequently include John Clutterbuck's *A Plain and Rational Vindication and Explanation of the Liturgy* (1694) and Thomas Bisse's *Two Letters in Defence of the English Liturgy and Reformation* (1717).

[16] W. D. Wilson (ed.), *Mant on the Rubrics: An Explanation of the Rubrics in the Book of Common Prayer, with Special Reference to Uniformity in Conducting the Service* (New York, 1847), p. 41.

[17] Ibid., p. 79.

[18] Mant would have agreed with William van Mildert, the future Bishop of Durham, who stated in a sermon of 1797, "Upon the preservation . . . of our excellent Liturgy in its present improved state, must depend, in a great measure, the preservation of the Church of England." See further, Bryan D. Spinks, *The Rise and Fall of the Incomparable Liturgy: The Book of Common*

Prayer, 1559–1906, Alcuin Club Collections, No. 92 (London: SPCK, 2017), p. 80.

[19] W. D. Wilson (ed.), *Mant on the Rubrics*, p. 19.

[20] Ibid., p. 106.

[21] Ibid., p. 169.

[22] In the 1820s and 1830s, under the influence of Bishop Charles Lloyd and later the leaders of the Oxford Movement, the study of medieval service books became widespread in Oxford. In Geoffrey Cuming's words, "Oxford became the source of a flood of liturgical reprints", culminating in the work of William Maskell (see Chapter 12) and others. See, G. J. Cuming, *A History of Anglican Liturgy* (2nd edn, London: Macmillan, 1982), p. 148.

[23] Wilson, *Mant on the Rubrics*, pp. 182–3.

[24] Wilson, Appendix to *Mant on the Rubrics*, p. 198.

[25] See further, *The Oxford Dictionary of the Christian Church*, 4th edn, ed. Andrew Louth (Oxford: Oxford University Press, 2022), Vol. 1, pp. 978–80, "Christianity in Ireland".

[26] See also Benjamin Crosby, "Read, Mark, Learn and Inwardly Digest: The Prayer Book and Private Devotion in Prayer Book Commentaries from Sparrow to Mant", *Journal of Anglican Studies* 21 (2023), pp. 87–105 (102): "This work [Mant's annotated *Prayer Book* of 1820] would prove, in retrospect, the high-water mark of the prayer book commentary tradition of the long eighteenth century. Mant produced a now-familiar genre of text: the Book of Common Prayer itself, annotated with abundant notes drawn from the commentary tradition."

[27] See p. 138, with particular reference to Thomas Frederick Simmons. Also, R. C. D. Jasper, *Prayer Book Revision in England, 1800–1900* (London: SPCK, 1954), pp. 121–7.

9

Charles Lloyd's unpublished Oxford lectures on the Book of Common Prayer (1823)

Even in the excessive and tiresome anti-Roman Catholic invective of Charles Wheatly, and in all of the eighteenth-century writings on the Book of Common Prayer, there is a pastoral note and a concern for the spiritual life of the Church of England and its members, both clerical and lay. C. J. Stranks in his book *Anglican Devotion* (1961) wrote:

> It was round the Prayer Book that the main body of Anglican piety was made to centre. England was to become a nation of churchmen once more. It was felt that if only people could be got to understand the nature and purpose of the Church's services they would come to love them and find them in every way sufficient. Its prayers offered the best stimulus for the Christian's most profound thoughts about his faith, selections from them, rearranged to suit personal needs, were the best possible manual of private devotion. Though many of those who wrote about the Prayer Book were learned in the history of liturgies it was not their main object to promote liturgical studies as such. They wished to show how closely the Prayer Book corresponded with the devotional temper and methods of the undivided Church, which was the standard to which Christian worship, in their opinion, should conform.[1]

The writings of the majority of the writers on the Prayer Book whom we have been following from Bishop Anthony Sparrow to Bishop Thomas

Wilson, were taken up by the leaders of the Oxford Movement as their natural forefathers in the Church, though a new tone was struck from the early years of the nineteenth century. The study of the Prayer Book moved, at least in part, from the rectories and episcopal palaces of the Church of England to the academic classrooms of the University of Oxford. This shift was due in large part to one man who was at once Bishop of Oxford and regius professor of divinity at Christ Church, Oxford—Charles Lloyd (1784–1829).

Charles Lloyd was the son of a poor clergyman and schoolmaster, Thomas Lloyd (1745–1815), his mother, Elizabeth (1760–1814), being one of three illegitimate children of Nathaniel Ryder (1735–1803), the first Baron Harrowby.[2] In a way, therefore, he was linked by family to the aristocracy, but grew up under his father's care and tutelage in scholarly but financially straitened conditions. Sent to Eton in 1800 at the age of 15, Charles was, then, hardly a privileged and wealthy pupil, being what was known as a "colleger", that is, a pupil who was supported by a foundation scholarship.[3] His time at school was not happy. From Eton he matriculated at Christ Church, Oxford in February 1803, beginning a relationship with the college that was to last for the remainder of his life. Graduating with first class honours in 1806, Lloyd briefly served as tutor of the children of Lord Elgin in Dunfermline before he returned to Oxford as mathematics tutor at Christ Church. He remained as a Student (Fellow) and tutor of Christ Church for nearly 20 years, his Studentship only ending when he was appointed regius professor of divinity and canon of Christ Church Cathedral in 1821, the year before his marriage to Mary Harriet Stapleton in 1822.

Becoming Bishop of Oxford five years later in 1827, a position which he held in conjunction with the regius professorship, Lloyd, once the college tutor of Robert Peel, became deeply involved with the political problems of Ireland and Catholic emancipation in the repeal of the Test and Corporation Acts, which had, since the seventeenth century, restricted government and municipal offices to members of the Church of England.[4] Lloyd's support for reform and for Catholic emancipation earned him the enmity of no less a figure than the King, George IV. Charles Lloyd never enjoyed robust health and died after a short illness in 1829.

Lloyd published little,[5] but he was a vastly influential teacher in Oxford, through his lectures in Christ Church directly affecting almost all the major figures of the Oxford Movement, including J. H. Newman, Richard Hurrell Froude, Frederick Oakeley, Robert and Isaac Wilberforce and G. A. Denison. In David Newsome's words, Lloyd was "a scholar whose painstaking exegesis and meticulous precision left their mark on his brilliant pupils who came to study under him in the 1820s".[6] But it was Edward Bouverie Pusey upon whom he had the greatest influence, encouraging Pusey to study theology in Germany. It was a radical suggestion in those days, but Lloyd was well aware that Oxford in his time was effectively incapable of appreciating (and therefore effectively opposing) the "critical" scholarship emerging from German universities. As H. P. Liddon in his great *Life of Pusey* (1894–98) pointed out, only two people in Oxford were then capable of even reading German—Dr Cardwell, the Principal of St Alban Hall,[7] and Mr Mill of Magdalen College.[8]

But it was in his private lectures of 1823 given in his rooms in Christ Church that Lloyd made his greatest impact on the future Oxford Movement and upon men like Newman, Pusey and Froude. The subject of the lectures was the history of the Book of Common Prayer, and Lloyd's own working Prayer Book, now in Christ Church Library, is covered in his copious marginal notes. One of the earliest historians of the Oxford Movement, R. W. Church, commented on these lectures that Lloyd

> had taught him [Froude] and others, to the surprise of many, that the familiar and venerated Prayer Book was but the reflection of medieval and primitive devotion, still embodied in its Latin forms in the Roman Service books; and so indirectly had planted in [his] mind the idea of the historical connexion, and in a very profound way the spiritual sympathy, of the modern with the pre-Reformation Church.[9]

It was hardly new teaching, as has been made clear in our studies of earlier Prayer Book commentators, but it was now raised to a new scholarly level with immediate and direct reference back to medieval liturgy in missals and breviaries from which Lloyd cited from frequently. Indeed, it was the teaching and scholarship of Lloyd that was to have a profound influence and effect not only on liturgical study, but also the scholarly (as opposed to "antiquarian") editing of medieval liturgical and religious texts in the nineteenth century. In Lloyd's notes, constant reference is made to the similarity of the Prayer Book to the Roman Missal (such phrases as "so in the Missal" and "the same as in the Missal" occur frequently) and the use or adaptation of the Breviary for the BCP as, for example, in the collect for the first Sunday in Lent.[10] (In fact, as a more recent and perhaps more discerning commentator, Bridget Nichols, has pointed out, this particular Prayer Book collect "is a decisive inversion of the thought of the rejected collect of the day in the Sarum Missal".[11]) Nevertheless, in the words of Lloyd's biographer William J. Baker:

> Citing often from the Salisbury Breviary, the liturgy of John Chrysostom, a French Missal, and the Sarum Missal, Lloyd compared the ancient liturgies not only with the changes effected during the Edwardian Reformation, but also with further minor alterations after the Savoy Conference of 1661.[12]

In the tradition of Charles Wheatly in the eighteenth century, and developed at much greater length by William Palmer in his *Origines Liturgicae* (1832), Lloyd traced the four great apostolic and primitive sources of the Prayer Book, that is, according to Wheatly, the liturgies of St Basil, St Chrysostom, St Ambrose and St Gregory.[13]

Lloyd's unpublished lectures on the origins of the Prayer Book lived on in the sermons and lectures of others in Oxford and far beyond in schools and parishes, and indeed well into the nineteenth century. One member of Lloyd's private class of 1823, George Moberly of Balliol College, later became headmaster of Winchester College (1835–66), where his pupils "listened to lectures on the same subject, delivered probably in the self-same words (if not even in the self-same manner) from the notes which the Doctor (Moberly) had entered in his prayer book in imitation of the method adopted by Lloyd".[14]

But it is in the work of William Palmer of Worcester College, Oxford that Lloyd's scholarship and teaching on the Prayer Book has been most fully preserved. Initially his papers were passed on to his successor as regius chair of divinity, Edward Burton, and then through him to William Palmer, and the result was his seminal work, *Origines Liturgicae*. (Palmer had himself previously been writing a commentary on the English liturgy but had abandoned it knowing that Lloyd, before his death, was also planning, at some stage, to publish the notes from his lectures.) As a study of the origins of the liturgy of the Church of England, Palmer's work self-confessedly owes almost everything of substance to Bishop Lloyd, and in his Preface Palmer, remarking that he has "been informed" of the private lectures for which the notes were composed, writes:

> The late Bishop of Oxford (DR. LLOYD), whose authority should have weight on such a subject, was so convinced of its expediency, that he was himself collecting materials for the purpose, which he intended to publish so soon as his avocations should permit. His Lordship's collections were entered on the margin of a folio Prayer-Book, in the library given by Dr. Allestree for the use of the Regius Professor of Divinity in this University; and having been kindly permitted to compare them with the results of my own investigations, I have derived from them several valuable observations, which are acknowledged in their proper places.[15]

These "several valuable observations" in fact constitute a significant part of the *Origines*, a substantial work in two parts, the first dealing with the "primitive" liturgies of the early Church and the second the "antiquities of the English Ritual", demonstrative of the 1,500 or so years of liturgical development that lie behind the Book of Common Prayer.

William Palmer was described by Newman in his *Apologia* (1864) as "the only really learned man among us",[16] but it should never be forgotten that behind Palmer stands the largely forgotten figure of Bishop Charles Lloyd, whose liturgical scholarship took the Church of England and its Prayer Book firmly into the nineteenth century and heralded the age of the scholarly editing of medieval manuscripts and texts, liturgical, religious and more and who, in the words of Dean Church, "if he had lived, would have played a considerable part" in the Oxford Movement, whose young minds he had done so much to form.

Notes

1   C. J. Stranks, *Anglican Devotion: Studies in the Spiritual Life of the Church of England between the Reformation and the Oxford Movement* (London: SCM Press, 1961), pp. 172–3.

2   J. F. A. Mason, "Charles Lloyd, Bishop of Oxford 1827–9, and his Family", *Oxoniensia* LXV (2000), pp. 447–51 (448).

3   William J. Baker, *Beyond Port and Prejudice: Charles Lloyd of Oxford, 1784–1829* (Orono, ME: University of Maine Press, 1981), p. 8.

4   Ibid., pp. 169–99. The Corporation Act was passed in 1661, and the Test Acts in 1673 and 1678.

5   His principal work was an edited volume entitled *The Formularies of Faith put forth by Authority during the Reign of Henry VIII* (Oxford, 1825). Within this book were important new editions of two key Reformation documents of the reign of Henry VIII, *The Bishops' Book* (1537) and its later revision, *The King's Book* (1543).

6   David Newsome, *The Parting of Friends* (London: John Murray, 1966), p. 78.

7   See further on Edward Cardwell, Chapter 11.

8   H. P. Liddon, *Life of Pusey* (1894–8), Vol. I. (4th edn, London: Longmans, Green and Co., 1894), p. 72.

9   R. W. Church, *The Oxford Movement: Twelve Years, 1833–1845* [1891] (Chicago: University of Chicago Press, 1970), p. 38.

10   "O Lord, who for our sake didst fast forty days and forty nights; Give us grace to use such abstinence, that, our flesh being subdued to the Spirit, we may ever obey thy godly motions in righteousness, and true holiness, to thy honour and glory, who livest and reignest with the Father and the Holy Ghost, one God, world without end. Amen."

11   Bridget Nichols (ed.), *The Collect in the Churches of the Reformation* (London: SCM Press, 2010), p. 23. Nichols provides the Latin text of the Sarum collect: "*Deus qui ecclesiam tuam annua quadragesimali observatione purificas: presta familie tue vt quod a te obtinere abstinendo nititur: hoc bonis operibus exequatur. Per dominum.*" Nichols draws her text from F. E. Brightman, *The English Rite*. Vol. 1 (London: Rivingtons, 1915), p. 294.

12   Baker, *Beyond Port and Prejudice*, p. 214.

76 THE BOOK OF COMMON PRAYER AND ITS COMMENTATORS

[13]   R. C. D. Jasper, *The Development of the Anglican Liturgy, 1662–1980* (London: SPCK, 1989), p. 42. After Lloyd, Jasper suggests, the "origins [of the BCP] were much richer and more diverse than many writers had imagined it".

[14]   W. J. Copeland, "History of the Oxford Movement" (MS in Pusey House), II, pp. 73–4.

[15]   William Palmer, *Origines Liturgicae, or, Antiquities of the English Ritual and a Dissertation on Primitive Liturgies* (4th edn, London: Francis & John Rivington, 1845), Vol. I, pp. vi–vii.

[16]   See further, Chapter 10.

1 0

William Patrick Palmer, *Origines Liturgicae* (1832)

William Patrick Palmer was born in Dublin, on 14 February 1803, of a military family. He was educated at Trinity College, Dublin, graduating in 1824, and he was tutored and later ordained as an Anglican priest by the High Church John Jebb, Bishop of Limerick. Jebb and his teacher, Alexander Knox,[1] were once credited with being the real originators of the Oxford Movement.[2] Palmer moved to Oxford in 1828, proceeding to his MA at Magdalen Hall[3] in 1829 and thence to a fellowship at Worcester College in 1831.

Palmer's interest in the primitive origins of the English liturgy, encouraged by Bishop Jebb, dates from as early as 1826. On the early death at the age of 44 of Bishop Charles Lloyd in 1829, Lloyd's unpublished lecture notes on the history and structure of the Book of Common Prayer, many of them annotations in his copy of the Prayer Book, passed to his pupil and successor as regius professor of divinity in Christ Church, Edward Burton, who in turn passed them on to Palmer. They formed the basis for Palmer's great work *Origines Liturgicae* (1832). This two-volume work on the origins of the BCP quickly attracted the attention of Hugh James Rose, a leader of the so-called "Hackney Phalanx",[4] and thereby Palmer was drawn into the beginnings of the Oxford Movement. Shy and reserved by nature, Palmer was described by J. H. Newman as "the only really learned man among us", though he was never a close associate of the inner group in Oxford. Indeed, in 1838, Newman wrote of Palmer to John William Bowden that "good fellow as he is, he has never been one of our own".[5]

In 1839, Palmer married Sophia Mary Bonne. Increasingly distanced from the Tractarians and Newman (who in his *Apologia Pro Vita Sua* [1864] described Palmer somewhat dismissively as among "a board of safe, sound sensible men"), Palmer eventually left Oxford to take up a career as a parish priest, becoming in 1846 the vicar of the distinctly Trollopian parish of Whitchurch Canonicorum in Dorset, with its ancient church of St Candida and Holy Cross, known locally as the Cathedral of the Vale.[6] Perhaps significantly, there is little record of his 23 years' service in this benefice, though his later writings suggest a devotion to the pastoral and parochial ministry of the church.[7] In his work and ministry in his remote and small parish,[8] Palmer seems to have lived out the Tractarian doctrine of reserve, and certainly he never courted attention and no biography has ever been written of him. Thomas Mozley was later to write that Palmer never sought rewards, which "he wanted not, but he had not even recognition".[9] After his retirement on the grounds of ill health in 1869, Palmer moved to London, where somewhat oddly, given his modest nature, he expended considerable energy in asserting his claim to the disputed baronetcy of Wingham, Kent. Almost certainly improperly he assumed the title of Sir William Palmer from 1865 and is deferentially addressed as such by J. H. Blunt in the Preface to his *Annotated Book of Common Prayer* (1866).[10]

Although its originality was questioned even at the time of its publication, *Origines Liturgicae* was undoubtedly one of the most influential liturgical publications of the nineteenth century. Following earlier writers like Charles Wheatly and others whom we have met in earlier chapters, Palmer seeks to establish the apostolic continuity of the English Church through the mission of Augustine of Canterbury, stating that:

> Although our liturgy and other offices were corrected and improved, chiefly after the example of the ancient Gallican, Spanish, Alexandrian, and Oriental, yet the greater proportion of our prayers have been continually retained and used by the church of England for more than twelve hundred years.[11]

For the Oxford Movement the establishment of this liturgical continuity in the Prayer Book was a central plank in their ecclesiology and understanding of the Church of England as firmly part of the universal catholic Church. In their hands, this ecclesiology became more refined than in previous centuries of the Church of England.

Origines Liturgicae is divided into two parts. The first, comprising essentially the first volume and entitled "Dissertation on Primitive Liturgies", examines 11 "liturgies" of the ancient Church identified by place, beginning with Antioch and Caesarea, and continuing to Constantinople, Alexandria, Ephesus, Rome and Milan, and including four very broad categories—Africa, Gaul, Spain, and Britain and Ireland. To the initial 11 "primitive liturgies" there are three "additions"—the liturgy of Armenia, Nestorian liturgies and Indian liturgies. Palmer frequently refers to the work of earlier, largely French, liturgical scholars such as Le Brun and Renaudot[12] as providing more detail than he himself gives.

The much larger second part of *Origines Liturgicae* is entitled "Antiquities of the English Ritual", describing the ancestry and pre-Reformation history of the Book of Common Prayer and concluding with brief comments on such occasional ceremonies and matters as the installation of deans, the coronation of monarchs, the blessing of military banners and the consecration of churches and cemeteries. *Origines* concludes with an illustrated description of the history and form of vestments, entitled "On Ecclesiastical Vestures". Throughout, Palmer, like those before him, repeatedly insists on the ancient roots of Prayer Book worship. Thus in his introduction to the office of Morning Prayer, he begins, typically, with the words, "First, let us consider the antiquity of the hours of prayer."[13] He then at some length traces the origin of the canonical hours to as early as the fourth century in Egypt, with Pachomius, Anthony and others of the Desert Fathers.

Throughout his work, Palmer was heavily dependent on earlier British and European (mainly French Benedictine) liturgical scholarship as well as the antiquarian resources of Joseph Bingham, Richard Gough, David Wilkins[14] and others. These antiquarian resources Palmer uses almost entirely uncritically, in contrast to the more meticulous William Maskell who, as we have already seen, is never slow to criticize the "most egregious blunders" of Gough and others.[15] In addition, Palmer draws on the work of L'Estrange, Wheatly and others in the English tradition of Prayer Book commentary. But also, usefully for later scholars, he provides extensive passages and excerpts from primary sources for the Prayer Book, such as lengthy Latin quotations from Cardinal "Quignon"'s Breviary, set alongside the text of the Preface to the 1549 Prayer Book. In short, *Origines* quickly became a valuable and much-used source in Prayer Book studies, such that Peter Knockles in his 2004 ODNB entry on Palmer simply states that *Origines* is (and the present tense remains) "by far the best book in the English language on the neglected theme of the history and significance of Anglican liturgical offices". He is possibly right, and the neglect of such careful historical studies has clearly had its negative effect on more recent exercises in Anglican liturgical revision.

Palmer, in the tradition of Wheatly and others, is quite clear that sound Anglican principles are to be distinguished from the errors of the "Romanists", and that the English Reformation was not a disturbance of the English Church's catholicity but rather a clearing away of Roman abuses and corruptions to reveal the more "primitive" forms of prayer within its liturgy.[16] He wrote:

> The English Prayer-Book was not composed within a few years, nor by a few men: it has descended to us with the improvements and the approbation of many centuries; and they who truly feel the calm and sublime elevation of our hymns and prayers, participate in the spirit of primitive devotion . . . There is scarcely a portion of our Prayer-Book which cannot in some way be traced to ancient offices.[17]

The second volume of *Origines* is substantially taken up with a commentary on "the Holy Communion, or Liturgy" (pp. 1–166), and Palmer is quite clear that the English medieval tradition of worship from which the Prayer Book descends is to be distinguished from that of Rome:

> It will be seen that Romanists are loud in their hostility to our liturgy, which in form and substance rather resembles the ancient

Gallican, Spanish, Egyptian, and Oriental liturgies than the Roman.[18]

In his defence of the Anglican theology and practice of Holy Communion, Palmer, essentially an historian, does betray himself at times as not being at heart either a theologian or true liturgiologist. This was, perhaps, the roots of Newman's hesitations about him. For example, his comments on the place of prayers for the departed in the prayer of consecration and oblation are, at best hesitant, and he is not entirely clear—as later commentators like Blunt or Frere certainly were absolutely clear—about the theological differences between the Prayer Books of 1549 and 1552. Nor is his comment on the absence of the epiclesis, the invocation of the Holy Spirit, in the Prayer Book totally convincing:

> I argue . . . that it is not essential to pray expressly for the Holy Ghost to sanctify the elements; because it is not essential in prayer to mention to God the means by which he is to accomplish the end which we pray for.[19]

This seems to be unsatisfactory on a number of levels, not least that of suggesting a kind of instrumentalism in the workings of the Almighty.

Nevertheless, we should not underestimate the importance of *Origines Liturgicae* in Prayer Book studies in the nineteenth century. Palmer's later career shows, however, that he was essentially, like Edward Cardwell, an ecclesiastical historian and an Anglican churchman whose moderation finally separated him from his Oxford friends, above all Newman. Perhaps Newman himself never quite understood the parochial and pastoral roots of the Church of England of which the BCP was the essential rock and foundation. Palmer recorded the parting of the ways from his Oxford colleagues in his 1843 publication entitled *A Narrative of Events Connected with the Publication of the Tracts for the Times, with Reflections on Existing tendencies to Romanism, and on the Present Duties and Prospects of Members of the Church.*

Apart from *Origines Liturgicae*, Palmer's chief work was his two-volume *Treatise on the Church of Christ, Designed Chiefly for the Use of Students in Theology* (1838). Described by Peter Nockles as "magisterial",

Palmer's undeniably dry style in the *Treatise* provoked a somewhat sardonic comment from Newman that it might be regarded as merely "a useful reference book for facts and nothing more". Nevertheless the *Treatise on the Church of Christ* provides perhaps the clearest articulation of the "branch theory" of the Church, whereby the Church of England is described as a legitimate branch of the Church catholic alongside and distinct from the Roman and Greek traditions.[20] The Prayer Book was the fundamental stem of this Anglican "catholicism".

William Palmer was, by all accounts, a gentle and humble man, a devoted servant of the Church of England and opponent of "Romanism". The latter earned him the enmity of the convert to Roman Catholicism, Peter le Page Renouf,[21] a man given to argument and animosity, in his pamphlet *The Character of the Rev. W. Palmer M.A. of Worcester College, as a Controversialist, Particularly with Reference to His Charge Against the Right Rev. Dr. Wiseman, of Quoting as Genuine Works of the Fathers, Spurious and Heretical Productions* (1843). Renouf, with considerable vindictiveness, accuses Palmer of selective and improper use of sources in his arguments, warning his readers against "implicit reliance on his authority".[22] While it is true that Palmer could not be called an original scholar, Renouf's judgment is harsh and did not finally detract from the importance and wide use of *Origines Liturgicae*. In later life in London, and after his retirement from parochial duties, Palmer made some contribution to the debate over "Vaticanism" in his pamphlet *Results of the 'Expostulation' of the Rt. Hon W. E. Gladstone in their Relation to the Unity of Roman Catholicism* (1875) but publishing only under the cover of a pseudonym "Umbra Oxoniensis".

And indeed, he was in a real sense a shadowy figure—a shade of Oxford who disappeared into country ministry. Yet though largely forgotten in the Oxford Movement to which he contributed so much in his liturgical work, Palmer remains still an important figure in the history of the Book of Common Prayer and its scholarly revival in the later nineteenth-century Church of England.

Notes

[1] Alexander Knox (1757–1831) was an Irish lay theologian who led a largely retired life near Dublin. His high theology of sacraments underlies all his work.

[2] See David Jasper and Jeremy J. Smith, *Reinventing Medieval Liturgy in Victorian England: Thomas Frederick Simmons and the Lay Folks' Mass Book* (Woodbridge: The Boydell Press, 2023), p. 36.

[3] He has sometimes been wrongly confused with another William Palmer (1811–79), of Magdalen College, also a High Church clergyman and theologian, who later converted to the Roman Catholic Church.

[4] A loosely defined group of High Church Anglicans, so called in distinction to the Evangelical Clapham Sect.

[5] John Henry Newman, *Letters and Diaries, 1837–1838*, Vol. 6, ed. Gerard Tracey (Oxford: Oxford University Press, 1984), p. 337.

[6] The relics of St Candida remain still undisturbed in the church. She is otherwise known as St Wite—hence the name of the village.

[7] Palmer is not named by George Herring among his list of the "Tractarian clergy from 1840–1870" in *The Oxford Movement in Practice: The Tractarian Parochial World from the 1830s to the 1870s* (Oxford: Oxford University Press, 2016).

[8] The population of Whitchurch Canonicorum today is 684.

[9] Thomas Mozley, *Reminiscences, Chiefly of Oriel College and the Oxford Movement*, 2 vols (Boston: Houghton, Mifflin and Co., 1882), Vol. 1, p. 322.

[10] See p. 131, Note 12.

[11] William Palmer, *Origines Liturgicae, or, Antiquities of the English Ritual and a Dissertation on Primitive Liturgies* (4th edn, London: Francis & John Rivington, 1845), Vol. 1, p. 189. See also, R. C. D. Jasper, *The Development of the Anglican Liturgy, 1662–1980* (London: SPCK, 1989), pp. 41–2.

[12] Jean-Baptiste le Brun des Marettes (1651–1731) was the author of *Voyages Liturgiques de France* (1718). Eusebius Renaudot (1648–1720) was trained by the Jesuits in Paris and became one of the greatest Orientalists and liturgical scholars of his time.

[13] Palmer, *Origines Liturgicae*, Vol. 1, p. 201.

[14] See Chapter 4.

84 THE BOOK OF COMMON PRAYER AND ITS COMMENTATORS

[15] William Maskell, *Monumenta Ritualia Ecclesiae Anglicanae* (2nd edn, Oxford: Clarendon Press, 1882), Vol. 1, p. x. See also Chapter 12 on William Maskell.

[16] Palmer would not, however, have agreed with Hurrell Froude's notorious suggestion, recorded in his *Remains* (1838), that the English Reformation "was a limb badly set; it must be broken again in order to be righted".

[17] Palmer, *Origines Liturgicae*, Vol. 1, p. vi.

[18] Ibid., Vol. 2, p. 2. More recent Anglican liturgical scholarship has been eager to reject this widely held Victorian liturgical principle of the distinctiveness of the English medieval liturgical tradition. Writing on the work of the later Roman Catholic liturgist Edmund Bishop, Matthew Cheung Salisbury has commented rather tartly, "Bishop rightly understood that the Anglican, mainly High Church, preoccupation with discovering the origin and nature of 'Sarum Use' was caused by the aspiration that the Church of England, and its liturgy, had an ancient and noble origin equal to and distinct from the Roman Rite as it had developed in continental Europe. This of course is not true, and Bishop knew it." *Worship in Medieval England* (Leeds: ARC Humanities Press, 2018), pp. 30–1. This may be true, but the point is still worth returning to.

[19] Palmer, *Origines Liturgicae*, Vol. 2, p. 138.

[20] A later prominent champion of the "branch theory" of catholicism was Darwell Stone (1859–1941), author of *The Christian Church* (1905) and the still useful *History of the Doctrine of the Holy Eucharist* (1909).

[21] Renouf converted under the influence of Newman and from 1855 to 1864 was Professor of Ancient History and Oriental Languages in Newman's Roman Catholic university in Dublin.

[22] Peter le Page Renouf, *The Character of the Rev. William Palmer as a Controversialist* (London: C. Dolman, 1843), p. 3.

1 1

Edward Cardwell, *The Two Books of Common Prayer* (1839)

Edward Cardwell was born in Standishgate, Wigan on 3 August 1787, the son of Richard Cardwell of Blackburn, Lancashire. He was educated at Brasenose College, Oxford, receiving his BA in 1809 and eventually his DD in 1831, and he spent his whole life in Oxford until his death, while still principal of St Alban Hall,[1] on 23 May 1861. In 1825, Cardwell was elected Camden professor of ancient history. He refused various church preferments, including the deanery of Carlisle Cathedral, offered to him by Sir Robert Peel, who was a personal friend, and much of his career in Oxford was spent in university administration and government, including playing a central role in the management of the Oxford University Press. Successive chancellors—Lord Grenville, the Duke of Wellington and Lord Derby—appointed him as their private secretary. No biography of him has been written.

But it is as an ecclesiastical historian that Cardwell is remembered today, his reputation in this field only outshone by William Palmer of Worcester College with his magisterial *Treatise on the Church of Christ* of 1838. Cardwell's early publications were in the field of classical studies, including an edition of Aristotle's *Ethics* (2 volumes, 1828–30) and his university lectures on ancient Greek and Latin coinage (1832). During the 1830s, however, and following the development of the Oxford Movement after 1833 (to the principles of which he was opposed), Cardwell pursued an interest in the documentary history of the Church of England, primarily in the sixteenth and seventeenth centuries. His initial focus was on the Book of Common Prayer.

86   THE BOOK OF COMMON PRAYER AND ITS COMMENTATORS

In 1839, Cardwell published his *Documentary Annals of the Reformed Church of England* in two volumes, and, more significantly for our present purposes, *The Two Books of Common Prayer, Set Forth by Authority of Parliament in the Reign of King Edward the Sixth: Compared with Each Other*. In this comparison between the Edwardine Prayer Books of 1549 and 1552, Cardwell writes primarily as an historian rather than either a liturgist[2] or theologian. Thus, for example, the central debate over the question of the Real Presence in the sacramental elements of Holy Communion he almost summarily dismisses as being "of small compass, and of secondary importance".[3] In the early history of the Anglican Prayer Book, Cardwell tends to downplay the role of European Protestant scholars such as Martin Bucer, Peter Martyr and Melanchthon in favour of what he describes as the "clearer perception" of Archbishop Cranmer and others in England, though his emphasis is always on the political and parliamentary rather than the theological circumstances of the Church and its liturgy, writing that

> the spirit promoted by these zealous foreigners was already in full activity in the minds of the English reformers, although in their case, it was united with a clearer perception of the difficulties in their way.[4]

Theological debates and questions are treated by Cardwell with a somewhat detached lack of detail. For example, on the arguments relating to the exclusion of the epiclesis and the separation of the prayer of oblation from the prayer of consecration in the 1552 Prayer Book, Cardwell writes:

> The Communion Service of the first Liturgy [1549] contained a prayer for the descent of the Holy Spirit upon the bread and wine, and a following prayer of oblation, which, together with the form of words addressed to the communicants, were designed to represent a sacrifice, and appeared to undiscriminating minds to denote the sacrifice of the mass. Numerous, therefore, and urgent were the objections against this portion of the service. Combined with a large class of objectors, whose theology consisted merely

in an undefined dread of Romanism, were all those, however differing among themselves, who believed the holy communion to be a feast and not a sacrifice, and that larger class of persons, who, placing the solemn duty upon its proper religious basis, were contented to worship without waiting to refine.[5]

Given the growing theological sophistication in such matters among Tractarian theologians in his time,[6] Cardwell's tone seems dry, descriptive and almost dismissive of theological niceties. He was, however, clear in his view about the establishment of "pure religion" in the early English Reformation under Henry VIII, as opposed to the "flagrant corruptions" of the Roman Catholic tradition.[7]

Cardwell was an historian who placed great emphasis on the value of contemporary sources. He is careful in his choice of texts for the two Prayer Books,[8] and apart from texts and documents in the British Museum and the Bodleian Library, draws upon the resources of such authors as Peter Heylyn, Bishop Sparrow, Hamon L'Estrange and, above all, David Wilkins (1685–1745) and his vast collection of ecclesiastical documents entitled *Concilia Magnae Britanniae et Hiberniae* (4 volumes, 1737), using almost exclusively the fourth volume of this work covering the years 1546 to 1717.[9]

In 1840, Cardwell published what he described as a sequel to *The Two Books of Common Prayer*, his *History of Conferences and Other Proceedings connected with the Revision of the Book of Common Prayer; from the Year 1558 to the Year 1690*. "The two volumes jointly", he wrote as a Preface, "are intended to contain a complete documentary history of the English Liturgy from the period of the Reformation down to the present time." The book is largely a collection of papers and proceedings, once again drawing heavily on previous antiquarian transcriptions such as those of Wilkins, beginning with the reign of Elizabeth I, through the Hampton Court Conference of January 1604 up to the Savoy Conference of 1661, the publication of the 1662 Prayer Book and Commission of William and Mary for the Review of the Liturgy in 1689. Cardwell's dislike of the "Court of Rome" is matched only by his distaste for Puritans and Nonconformists, while Edward VI, on the other hand, he wrote approvingly, "had adopted the principles of the Reformation to a greater

88   THE BOOK OF COMMON PRAYER AND ITS COMMENTATORS

extent and in a more religious spirit than most of his contemporaries".[10] While he does identify the two central issues within the practice and theology of the Church of "the proper use of clerical vestments" and the question of the Real Presence in the Eucharist,[11] Cardwell chooses to focus primarily upon the political and power issues relating to the debates over the liturgy of the Prayer Book, with little detail given to textual and liturgical matters. For example, in his commentary on the process leading up to the authorization of the 1662 Prayer Book—with but passing references to the work of Bishop Cosin and others in *The Durham Book*[12]—Cardwell writes in general and unspecific tones:

> The fear, which the commons seem to have contracted, that occasion would be taken for introducing into the Liturgy the *religious sentiments* of archbishop Laud and *his school of theologians*, was not altogether without foundation.[13]

This suggestion he links to the common assumption, now widely questioned,[14] that the influential (though little actually used) Scottish Prayer Book of 1637 was made on largely Laudian principles.

Cardwell concludes his book, *A History of Conferences*, with the question to the Church of his own time as to "whether it is necessary or desirable to make any further attempt at revising the Book of Common Prayer".[15] By 1840, not least under the influences of the *Tracts for the Times*, the matter of the Book of Common Prayer and the desirability of its revision was in the air of the Church of England.[16] William van Mildert's remark, made in 1797, that "upon the preservation ... of our excellent Liturgy in its present improved state, must depend, in a great measure, the preservation of the Church of England", was, some 40 years later, at least questionable and liturgical change was in the air.[17] Cardwell, however, remained hesitant about any liturgical reform of the Prayer Book, though his reasons were, to some extent at least, more practical and pragmatic rather than pastoral and theological: quite simply the Church of England's system of church government made change in the authorized liturgy practically impossible. Cardwell writes:

> To the further question whether a revision is desirable, an answer must be sought not so much from the general principles of a ritual, or the wants of a mixed congregation, as from the practical difficulties inseparable from such an undertaking.[18]

It was an odd argument. If later history would eventually find ways of making revisions through the labyrinthine processes of the Church and state government, Cardwell suggests that any passage through three separate assemblies, both ecclesiastical and civil, "a commission, a convocation, and a parliament . . . would seem to be almost unattainable".[19] And indeed, such bureaucratic immobility, he suggests, might even be the proper condition for the right stability of the Church of England against its detractors, as he looks back into the tempestuous history of the Anglican Church in the seventeenth century and "the rash proceedings of the Non-conformists, who had caused the flood-gates of enquiry to be thrown open, and were the first to be carried away by the torrent".[20] Cardwell was, in the end, an administrator who valued stability above all else. The more profound niceties of doctrine or pastoral demands did not seem to trouble him unduly.

Cardwell's only later major publication was another collection of historical documents, his two-volume work entitled *Synodalia: A Collection of Articles of Religion, Canons, and Proceedings of Convocations in the Province of Canterbury, from the Year 1547 to the Year 1717* (1842). An invaluable historical source book, though once again relying heavily on earlier antiquarian works by Wilkins, Joseph Bingham and others, Cardwell's *Synodalia* remained a standard textbook of Church history for over a century, until finally superseded by Gerald Bray's *The Anglican Canons, 1529–1947*, published by the Church of England Record Society in 1998. The documents in *Synodalia*, together with Cardwell's critical notes, were, he wrote,

> intended to supply a knowledge of the motives and details that constitute the living substance of history, without which the reader would in the present instance have had before him the bare skeleton of the church, considered in its jurisprudence, and have been unable to form any conjecture as to its animation or activity.[21]

Edward Cardwell's labours in Church historiography provided the later nineteenth-century Church of England with generally solid documentary foundations for the study of the Book of Common Prayer during the early English Reformation and into the seventeenth century. With the essence and pastoral spirit of the BCP, he seems little concerned.

Having said that, Cardwell's Editor's Preface to his volume on the Prayer Books of 1549 and 1552 is a clear and scholarly account of the early English Reformation from the perspective of a moderate evangelical. Like Bishop Mant before him, he has a clear preference for the Prayer Book of 1552 and its revisions, dismissing the "undiscriminating minds" of those who adhere to a belief in the "sacrifice of the mass".[22] Cardwell is clearly attracted to the revisions proposed by Martin Bucer and the Zwinglian theology of those "who looked upon the oblation of the Eucharist as consisting merely of prayer, thanksgiving, and the remembrance of our Saviour's passion".[23] Of disputes in the Church he broadly concludes that there is always a larger body of people whom theological argument leaves untroubled and who worship with the BCP "with undisturbed devotion". This may be true, but it does beg a large number of questions. Cardwell ends his Preface to *The Two Books of Common Prayer* with these words:

> There have always been, and probably will always continue, two opposite parties, who though devotedly attached to the doctrines of the church, have sought for a new revision of the Liturgy; the one, as was the case at the beginning of the last century, desiring that the prayers of consecration and oblation should be restored,[24] and the words 'militant here on earth'[25] should be expunged; the other complaining that the rights of conscience and of Christian liberty were invaded, and the means of religious usefulness curtailed. Happy is it for the church that there has always been between these opposite parties a much larger body of worshippers, who have used their Book of Common Prayer with undisturbed affection, offering thanks to God continually for his unspeakable gift.[26]

In a way, history has proved Cardwell correct. Sacramental and theological debate as regards Prayer Book revision never went away—at least, arguably, until the middle years of the twentieth century, after the time of Bishop Frere when Prayer Book revision, on a much more ecumenical basis, began to look much more like Prayer Book replacement. And almost certainly the large majority of those who faithfully worship with the BCP are little concerned about such matters. That does, however, raise fundamental questions about liturgical theology and its place—and with that we turn to a rather tougher figure than Cardwell—William Maskell.

Notes

[1] Established in the thirteenth century, St Alban Hall was acquired by Merton College in the sixteenth century and the two institutions merged in 1882 following a University Statute in 1881, when its members were admitted to Merton. Cardwell was appointed as Principal in 1831 in succession to Richard Whately. For a time under Whately, J. H. Newman was the Hall's Vice-Principal.

[2] The OED makes little distinction between its definitions of "liturgist" and "liturgiologist". The latter was used in the previous chapter with reference to William Palmer and denotes a more detached perspective on the liturgy.

[3] Edward Cardwell, *The Two Books of Common Prayer* (2nd edn, Oxford: Oxford University Press, 1841), p. xxiv. The doctrine of the Real Presence was a central issue in Tractarian debate and theology. See Alf Härdelin, *The Tractarian Understanding of the Eucharist* (Uppsala: Uppsala University, 1965), pp. 148–68.

[4] Ibid., p. xii.

[5] Ibid., p. xxvi–xxvii.

[6] See Härdelin, *The Tractarian Understanding of the Eucharist*, especially "The Eucharistic Presence", pp. 129–219.

[7] Cardwell, *The Two Books of Common Prayer*, pp. v and vii.

[8] See Caldwell's lengthy "Notes to the Second Edition", *The Two Books of Common Prayer*, pp. xl–xliv.

[9] On David Wilkins and *Concilia Magnae Britanniae*, Book IV, see Chapter 4.

[10] Edward Cardwell, *A History of Conferences* (2nd edn, Oxford: Oxford University Press, 1841), p. 2.

92   THE BOOK OF COMMON PRAYER AND ITS COMMENTATORS

[11]   Ibid., p. 3.

[12]   See G. J. Cuming, *The Durham Book: Being the First Draft of Revision of the B.C.P. in 1661* (Oxford: Oxford University Press, 1961).

[13]   Cardwell, *A History of Conferences*, p. 389 (emphases added).

[14]   See Gordon Donaldson, *The Making of the Scottish Prayer Book of 1637* (Edinburgh: Edinburgh University Press, 1954).

[15]   Cardwell, *A History of Conferences*, p. 460.

[16]   See R. C. D. Jasper, *Prayer Book Revision in England: 1800–1900* (London: SPCK, 1954).

[17]   See Bryan D. Spinks, *The Rise and Fall of the Incomparable Liturgy: The Book of Common Prayer, 1559–1906* (London: SPCK, 2017), p. 80, quoting from van Mildert's sermon of 25 April 1797, *The Excellency of the Liturgy and the Advantage of being Educated in the Doctrine and Principles of the Church of England* (London, 1797), p. 15. See also p. 68, Note 18, with reference to Bishop Mant.

[18]   Cardwell, *A History of Conferences*, p. 461.

[19]   Ibid., p. 461. As Cardwell wrote these words in 1840, it might be noted that neither the convocations of Canterbury or York had then met for more than one hundred years. The Convocation of Canterbury only reconvened in the nineteenth century in 1852 (and York in 1861).

[20]   Cardwell, *A History of Conferences*, p. 464.

[21]   Edward Cardwell, *Synodalia* (Oxford: Oxford University Press, 1842), Vol. 1, p. xxx.

[22]   Cardwell, *The Two Books of Common Prayer*, p. xxvi.

[23]   Ibid., pp. xxviii–xxix.

[24]   From the form of 1552 (as retained in 1662) to the original Cranmerian form of 1549.

[25]   The revision that thus removed prayers for the dead from the liturgy by the addition of the words "here on earth".

[26]   Cardwell, *The Two Books of Common Prayer*, pp. xxxvi–xxxvii.

1 2

William Maskell, *The Ancient Liturgy of the Church of England* (1844)

William Maskell (1814–1890) is an elusive and somewhat anomalous figure in the history of the nineteenth-century Church of England and liturgical scholarship primarily in the pre-Reformation period and the Book of Common Prayer. Described by Richard W. Pfaff as "one of the first scholars of the nineteenth century to devote himself to serious liturgical study",[1] Maskell remains largely unknown except amongst liturgical specialists today, his scholarly work balanced between the enthusiasm of an antiquary and the work of a serious and rather isolated scholar. No biography of his life has ever been written. Like others before him, Maskell's rather argumentative character did not serve him well.

Born the son of a solicitor in Shepton Mallet, Somerset, Maskell matriculated at University College, Oxford in 1832, graduating with a BA in 1836 (MA, 1838). Although from the time of his ordination into the Church of England in 1839 he identified with High Church views, as a liturgical scholar, despite his Oxford education, he set himself apart from Tractarian principles of liturgical revision that were built on the basis of the pastoral limitations of the Book of Common Prayer in a changing Church.[2] He might better be described as an old-fashioned High Churchman harking back to an earlier era in the Church of England. A man of a rather disputatious temperament and scholarly inclination, Maskell resigned the living of Corscombe, Dorset in 1842 after less than a year in order to devote himself to his scholarly work on what were to be his two great books: *The Ancient Liturgy of the Church of England According to the Uses of Sarum, York, Hereford and Bangor and the Roman Liturgy, arranged in parallel columns with Preface and Notes*

(1844; second edition, 1846; third edition, 1882); and the three massive volumes of the *Monumenta Ritualia Ecclesiae Anglicanae: The Occasional Offices of the Church of England according to the old use of Salisbury, the Prymer in English, and other prayers and forms with dissertations and notes* (1846; second edition, 1882). They were to remain his primary, indeed almost his only contributions to liturgical scholarship. Both were substantially revised towards the end of Maskell's life and are now better known in the editions of 1882.

On the recommendation of Bishop Denison of Salisbury, Maskell became domestic chaplain to the redoubtable Bishop Henry Phillpotts of Exeter, and vicar of St Mary's Church, Torquay in 1847. In the same fateful year, the Lord Chancellor offered the Revd George Cornelius Gorham the Crown living of Brampton Speke in the diocese of Exeter. The countersignature by the Bishop of Exeter, necessary for Gorham's induction, was withheld, however, on the grounds, and in the words of Bishop Phillpotts, that

> the Reverend George Cornelius Gorham did, in the course of the last year, in correspondence with myself, hold, write, and maintain what is contrary to the discipline of the said Church, and as what he further wrote makes me apprehend that he holds also what is contrary to its doctrine, I cannot conscientiously countersign his testimonial.[3]

The history of the notorious "Gorham Case" is labyrinthine, complex and well documented,[4] a crucial moment in the history of the debate upon Erastianism in the Victorian Church of England. It began with an examination of Gorham by Bishop Phillpotts consisting of no less than 149 questions, largely related to the doctrine of baptismal regeneration. Gorham's statement that, in baptism, "where there is no worthy reception, there is no bestowment of grace",[5] failed to satisfy the sacramental principles of the High Church bishop. But this doctrinal argument was not to be the nub of the affair, nor indeed the matter for the primary involvement of Maskell in it. When, in 1849, the Court of Arches ruled in favour of the bishop, the Dean of Arches—Sir Herbert Jenner Fust—concluding that Gorham "does maintain opinions opposed to that

Church of which he professes himself a member and minister",[6] Gorham immediately appealed to the Judicial Committee of the Privy Council, which, in 1850, overturned the decision of the Court of Arches. Such was the notoriety of this essentially "secular" decision that it remained a matter of lengthy discussion by Lytton Strachey over half a century later in his book *Eminent Victorians* (1918), writing, in his essay on Cardinal Manning, an Anglican archdeacon at the time of the Gorham case, of the decision of the Judicial Committee and indeed its continuing significance:

> Whether his [Gorham's] views were theologically correct or not, they said, was not their business; it was their business to decide whether the opinions under consideration were contrary or repugnant to the doctrine of the Church of England as enjoined upon the clergy by its Articles, Formularies, and Rubrics; and they had come to the conclusion that they were not. The judgment still holds good; and to this day a clergyman of the Church of England is quite at liberty to believe that regeneration does not invariably take place when the infant is baptised.[7]

Maskell, whose fate was not to be entirely distinguished from Manning's as a consequence of this judgment, was at this time Bishop Phillpott's domestic chaplain and in this capacity closely involved in the matter of Gorham. Indeed, it was clear that the bishop and his chaplain shared similar High Church views on the matter of the sacraments of baptism and Eucharist, views that were clearly expressed by Maskell in a volume of his sermons published in 1849. Significantly Maskell went further as a High Churchman in an attempt to revive the practice of the confessional in his pamphlet *An Enquiry into the Doctrine of the Church of England upon Absolution* (1849). By then, however, his friendly relationship with his bishop was beginning to cool, finally disintegrating on Maskell's publication of his vitriolic *First Letter on the Present Position of the High Church Party in the Church of England: The Royal Supremacy, and the Authority of the Judicial Committee of the Privy Council* in 1850, written and published before the decision of the Judicial Committee on the matter of Gorham was pronounced. The tone of Maskell's *Letter* filled

96   THE BOOK OF COMMON PRAYER AND ITS COMMENTATORS

Phillpotts with "unmitigated disgust" and accordingly he wrote to his chaplain:

> That I write with pain I need not assure you. I cannot, and wish not to forget the, to me, very gratifying intercourse which has subsisted between us during the last three years. It has been on my part, more entirely open and unreserved than I have held with any other. I shall look back upon it with lasting regret—with regret incomparably more bitter than if I had mourned over your grave.[8]

In a further letter to Maskell, in which Phillpotts refuses his chaplain's offered resignation of his charge, the bishop remarked further with some puzzlement over the substance of Maskell's *First Letter*:

> That there is much of truth in what you say, I feel; that there is *so* much as you believe, I cannot assent. I regard your publication as one of the perplexing facts in our present state. May God enable us to deal with all of them in such a manner as shall be best for the Church![9]

The doctrinal and ecclesiological difference, in the end, between Maskell and Phillpotts was one of degree, indicative of the limits of the bishop's High Churchmanship and the relentlessly logical extent of Maskell's.

Maskell subsequently added a second letter to his first, publishing them together and much later in 1869 as *The Present Position of the High-Church Party in the Church Considered in a Review of the 'Civil Power in Its Relations with the Church' and in Two Letters on the Royal Supremacy and Want of Dogmatic Teaching in the Reformed Church*. By this time, Maskell was a Roman Catholic. But as, in 1850, the Gorham case proceeded from the Court of Arches to the Judicial Committee of the Privy Council, Maskell became less convinced that Gorham was doctrinally incorrect given his position in the Church of England. The difficulty for Maskell—as a Roman Catholic—was that he still disagreed with Gorham, and therefore he disagreed with the Church of England itself. In short, Gorham was wrong, *as an Anglican*. And so the decision of the Judicial Committee to overturn the ruling of the Court of Arches, which had been in favour of Bishop Phillpotts, was not so much wrong in its judgment upon the doctrine of the Church of England, it was wrong because it represented a profound flaw in the structures of authority (and therefore doctrine) within the Church itself. The difficulty rested upon the claims of "Royal Supremacy" since the time of Henry VIII. Maskell puts it thus in his *First Letter*:

> The title of supreme head arrogated to himself by Henry the eighth, and allowed and confirmed by repeated statutes during his reign, was altered into the somewhat less objectionable title "supreme governor" in the time of queen Elizabeth. It is positively incredible that Henry should have desired the title of supreme head to have been given to him, in the strict sense in which it belongs to our Blessed Lord ... the title, used in any way, was objectionable, and likely to be misunderstood.[10]

The Judicial Committee represented an errant secular jurisdiction over the spiritual and doctrinal affairs of the Church, being, in Maskell's words, "nothing more than the necessary organ of the Royal Supremacy as established by the statutes of Henry VIII and Elizabeth".[11]

It is not difficult to understand the distaste felt by Bishop Phillpotts for the manner in which Maskell's letter is written. Its language is at times excessive and even brutal. The spiritual affairs of the Church, wrote Maskell, are ruled over by an "irresponsible cabinet" while within the Church of England there is a sad "want of necessary dogmatic teaching".[12] This account of the Gorham case and Maskell's part in it provides a necessary background to his liturgical labours on the Uses of the late medieval and pre-Reformation English Church. Liturgy and the BCP are inextricably part of not only the doctrinal and pastoral but also the political life of the Church of England.

Thus it was against this energetic political background that Maskell pursued his liturgical studies in the medieval rites of the English Church and, thereby, the roots of the Book of Common Prayer. The study of liturgy, if more scholarly than in the previous century, was certainly not isolated from the wider business of the Church and its place in the life of the nation. There is a careful and precise manner of argument in the *Letter* that also characterizes Maskell's liturgical editing and gives it real substance. But it was precisely this that drove him out of the Church of England and towards Rome. In the aftermath of the Judicial Committee's ruling, given after the publication of the *First Letter*, Maskell was not prepared to distinguish between a ruling that was a matter of interpretation of doctrine, in which the Committee may well have been right in finding in favour of Gorham, and the Committee's power of declaring the truth or falseness of a doctrine.[13] The point was not that Gorham was wrong within the boundaries of the Church of England, but that the Church of England itself was wrong in its doctrine and therefore in its liturgy and public worship, and wrong furthermore inasmuch as it had allowed itself to be governed by an essentially secular Committee under the Crown, and had done so since the time of Henry VIII. In the words of the Church historian Peter Nockles, "In short, the Erastianism of 1850 was no different in kind from the Erastianism of 1530 as well as 1688."[14] It is necessary to appreciate this background, against which Maskell went back into the rituals and worship of the pre-Reformation and late medieval *Ecclesia Anglicana*.

Thus it was that in 1850 Maskell, along with Archdeacon Manning and others, felt that he had no logical option but to leave the Church of England, within which his loyalty had never been with the Tractarians to whom Bishop Phillpotts was appealing for advice, above all Pusey and Keble, but rather with the older High Churchmen like William Palmer, author of *Origines Liturgicae* (1832), and this, as we shall see, was significant for his work on the medieval English liturgy and the roots of the BCP.

In the wake of the Gorham case and with the advice of J. H. Newman, Maskell resigned his living of St Mary's Church, Torquay and was received into the Roman Catholic Church, publicizing his conversion in a *Letter to the Rev. Dr. Pusey on his receiving Persons in Auricular Confession* (1850). For the remaining 40 years of his life, he led the life of a country gentleman and scholar in some seclusion (although he was a Justice of the Peace and a deputy lieutenant for Cornwall) in Bude and finally Penzance, never taking priestly orders in his adopted church following his second marriage in 1852. Maskell's combative

WILLIAM MASKELL

tendencies never left him, however, as he joined Newman and others in his rejection of papal infallibility as dogmatically propounded at the First Vatican Council (1869–70).[15] On this he disagreed, and characteristically with some violence, with the now Cardinal Manning. In 1872, Maskell published a brief pamphlet entitled *Protestant Ritualists*, in which he returned to the Gorham judgment and the position of the Tractarian clergy within the Church of England.[16] He begins his Preface with a typically uncompromising statement:

> The argument here offered against the claims of the reformed Church of England to be regarded and accepted as a part of the true Church of Christ is directed chiefly, as the title explains, in opposition to the position taken by high churchmen and ritualists in the Establishment.[17]

Yet this publication, in addition to a further controversy over allegations made in Sabine Baring-Gould's biography of Maskell's friend, the highly eccentric poet and priest Robert Stephen Hawker,[18] that Hawker had secretly subscribed to Roman Catholicism while remaining as vicar of Morwenstow in Cornwall, suggests that Maskell held the Church of England in continuing affection despite his dogmatic rejection of its catholic credentials.

A man of some considerable personal wealth, which he inherited from his father, Maskell spent his last years as a country gentleman, collecting medieval service books and amassing a large personal library. In 1872, he edited a lengthy volume entitled *A Description of the Ivories, Ancient and Modern, in the South Kensington Museum*. It remains in print today.

But perhaps now we get at last to the heart of the matter in our present concerns. Maskell's antiquarian tendencies lie at the heart of his, at first glance, rather puzzling position as a liturgical scholar. That he was a serious liturgical scholar of medieval liturgies is undeniable, far more so than his predecessor William Palmer of Worcester College, Oxford, with whom he shared many characteristics. Palmer's hugely influential *Origines Liturgicae* was largely dependent, as we have seen, on the earlier work of Bishop Charles Lloyd, while Maskell in his *Ancient Liturgy of the Church of England* worked from original sources, if not always the most reliable of them.[19] But like Palmer, Maskell did not share the well-tried project, taken up by the Tractarians (and Camdenites[20]) of returning to the late medieval English rites simply in order to correct the mistakes of the Reformation and restore the Prayer Book to its place within a catholic liturgical tradition. Palmer in the *Origines* had affirmed "the absolute infallibility and perfection of the Prayer Book", and, at least in the first two editions of the *Ancient Liturgy* (1844 and 1846) and before his conversion to Roman Catholicism, Maskell agreed, even to the point of affirming that "the essentials of a valid consecration are to be found in the liturgy of 1552: much more than after the improvements, few though they be, which from time to time have been made in it, by the Bishops in the reigns of Elizabeth, and James, and Charles".[21] As an Anglican, he clearly did not entirely share the Tractarian preoccupation with the 1549 rite of the first Edwardine Prayer Book, to be taken up vigorously by ritualists and by liturgists like Bishop W. H. Frere in the later part of the nineteenth century. Indeed, Maskell's position was always one of the *continuity* and essential simplicity of the "English rite" as at the heart of the Anglican position, insisting in the 1846 edition of the *Ancient Liturgy* that "none would wish to be restored the trifling observances and the doubtful rites which the rubrics of the old service[22] enjoin", and that "it is our duty to . . . express our dislike to much still retained in the present Roman liturgy, but which we have not in our own".[23]

And yet within some four years of writing these words as an Anglican priest, Maskell converted to the Roman Catholic Church. Odd though this might seem, there is a certain consistency and even logic to which he was bound and which led him in the third and final edition of the *Ancient Liturgy* in 1882 to retain in the title the words "Church of England". What he insisted on was the continuity of the liturgy from the medieval period, but a continuity embraced not by the widespread Tractarian claim for the "catholicity" of the Anglican tradition,[24] but only through the Roman Catholic Church itself, which was finally for Maskell the true English Church in continuity with the medieval rites of Sarum, York, Hereford and so on. We find, then, that the Preface to the 1882 edition of the *Ancient Liturgy* was considerably revised from 1846, though the work itself remains essentially the same. Indeed, already Maskell's adherence to the medieval English rites as opposed to the uniformity of "Rome" was becoming outdated by the more precise scholarship of Edmund Bishop, also a Roman Catholic, and others.[25] As Maskell wrote in his 1882 Preface:

> It is not possible to say whether, if the reformation had not taken place bringing with it the new common Prayer book and other changes, we should still have retained in England the old uses of, at least, Sarum and York. We cannot be surprised that under the pressure of the penal laws during the seventeenth and eighteenth centuries the observance of the older rituals gradually gave way to the introduction of the Roman use. We may—and very reasonably—regret the fact; but a fact it is, and we have lost, probably for ever, many an ancient rite and ceremony, many a prayer and litany, which connected the rituals of Queen Mary's reign with the mass said, or the offices which were celebrated, not only by St. Augustine before king Ethelbert and his people, but by priests and bishops of the earlier British church.[26]

This was argued by Maskell long after his conversion to Roman Catholicism. At the end of the Preface in the 1882 third edition of *The Ancient Liturgy of the Church of England*, Maskell comments upon and laments the lack of liturgical scholarship amongst "the clergy of the reformed church of England" and, he adds, "nor did they care to recollect that the common prayer book now used in their church is founded upon and draws it origin from the very sources"[27] of which they are so blatantly ignorant. The liturgical ignorance of the clergy, it must be admitted, was affirmed some years later by Percy Dearmer in *The Parson's Handbook* (1899).[28] One might be tempted to wonder how much has changed today.

Maskell draws, like many other liturgical scholars of his day, upon the earlier French and largely Benedictine scholarly tradition of Jean Mabillon (1632–1707), Edmond Martène (1654–1739) and others, though he is generally scathing in his 1882 Preface to the second edition of the *Monumenta Ritualia Ecclesiae Anglicanae* of the English tradition of Prayer Book scholarship culminating in the work of Charles Wheatly in the eighteenth century and William Palmer in the nineteenth century, a tradition of which, essentially, he was himself a part. His criticism is especially harsh with respect to the more antiquarian tendencies of such scholars as Richard Gough (1735–1809). More recently Gough has been properly recognized for his substantial work on the medieval service books and liturgical practices of Sarum (Salisbury) in his *Anecdotes of British Topography*, first published in 1786 (second volume, 1799).[29] Maskell is utterly dismissive of this work, as we have already seen in Chapter 4, comparing Gough with the later (and certainly far more dilettante) antiquarian Thomas Frognall Dibdin (1776–1847), and accusing him of "egregious blunders", although, having achieved little so that "in proportion they have made few mistakes, and so in that way do not mislead".[30]

Yet Maskell himself, though important in late medieval liturgical scholarship at least in the earlier part of the nineteenth century, never shed some of the characteristics of earlier antiquarian studies. Learned as he was he remained largely a solitary figure both as an Anglican and as a Roman Catholic, irascible and argumentative and undisciplined by the growing editorial methods and scholarly importance of such bodies as the Early English Text Society (important, as we shall see for T. F. Simmons), the Surtees Society (important for William G. Henderson), and later the Henry Bradshaw Society, founded in the year of Maskell's death, 1890.[31] Maskell rarely uses library shelf marks to reference the manuscripts or books he is working from, often making them difficult to trace. Phrases such as "if I remember rightly", hardly appropriate to the precision of modern scholarship, are common in his prefaces and annotations.[32] Corrected on one occasion in the Bodleian Library by his fellow liturgical scholar Thomas Frederick Simmons, Maskell steadfastly ignored the intervention (which was legitimate) without comment.[33] His work on the English medieval uses was later overtaken in the nineteenth century by such scholars as F. H. Dickinson and his Burntisland edition of the Sarum Use and William Henderson and his Surtees edition of the York Use. Furthermore, although Maskell was perfectly well aware of the instability and diversity of medieval liturgical texts, he remained convinced that in each case there was a "perfect" form of the text which assiduous scholarship would eventually unearth. Even in his own time, editorial practice and scholarship, and not least liturgical scholarship, moved on from such a position.

Although Maskell's two most significant works, his *Ancient Liturgy of the Church of England* and his *Monumenta Ritualia Ecclesiae Anglicanae*, both first published in the first half of the nineteenth century, were significant enough to be republished in splendid editions by the Clarendon Press in 1882, by the end of his life Maskell seemed a remote and outdated figure in the world of liturgical scholarship, his isolated antiquarian tendencies ever more apparent in his collections of enamels and ivory carvings alongside his library of medieval service books. Unlike many amongst the Anglican clergy, he was never associated with the Early English Text Society or other such increasingly significant intellectual and academic bodies in the field of medieval and liturgical editing and scholarship. Nevertheless he remains a significant figure in the study of English liturgical history and the origins of the Book of Common Prayer.

William Maskell died, aged 76 and largely forgotten, in Penzance on 12 April 1890.

Notes

[1]   Richard W. Pfaff, *The Liturgy in Medieval England: A History* (Oxford: Oxford University Press, 2009), p. 9.

[2]   See Peter B. Nockles, *The Oxford Movement in Context: Anglican High Churchmanship, 1760–1857* (Cambridge: Cambridge University Press, 1997), p. 222.

[3]   Quoted in G. C. Davies, *Henry Phillpotts, Bishop of Exeter, 1778–1869* (London: SPCK, 1954), p. 231.

[4]   See, for example, the now old but still useful J. C. S. Nias, *Gorham and the Bishop of Exeter* (London: SPCK, 1951). More briefly, Owen Chadwick, *The Victorian Church*, Part 1 (3rd edn, London: Adam & Charles Black, 1971), pp. 250–9.

[5]   Quoted in G. C. Broderick and W. H. Fremantle, *A Collection of the Judgments of the Judicial Committee of the Privy Council in Ecclesiastical Cases relating to Doctrine and Discipline* (London: J. Murray, 1865), p. 68.

[6]   Broderick and Fremantle, *A Collection of Judgments*, p. 80.

[7]   Lytton Strachey, *Eminent Victorians* [1918] (London: Chatto & Windus, 1929), p. 47.

8   British Museum MSS, quoted in G. C. Davies, *Henry Phillpotts*, p. 259.

9   Quoted in G. C. Davies, *Henry Phillpotts*, pp. 259–60.

10   William Maskell, *A First Letter on the Position of the High Church Party* (London: William Pickering, 1850), p. 33.

11   Maskell, *A First Letter*, p. 9.

12   Maskell, *A First Letter*, pp. 27, 6.

13   Maskell, *A First Letter*, p. 41.

14   Peter Nockles, *The Oxford Movement in Context*, p. 98.

15   Maskell published a pamphlet on the subject, *What is the Meaning of the late Definition on the Infallibility of the Pope?* (1871).

16   The pamphlet was originally six papers published in *The Tablet*.

17   William Maskell, *Protestant Ritualists* (London: James Toovey, 1872), Preface.

18   Hawker had a reputation for extreme eccentricity. He was reputed to have dressed on one occasion as a mermaid and to have excommunicated one of his nine cats (which accompanied him to church) for mousing on Sunday.

19   Richard Pfaff lists these sources, noting Maskell's inferences, which were sometimes pure guesswork. *The Liturgy in Medieval England*, p. 458.

20   The Cambridge Camden Society was founded in 1839 by J. M. Neale and Benjamin Webb. From 1845 it was known as the Ecclesiological Society. William Camden was a sixteenth-century antiquarian and historian.

21   Maskell, *The Ancient Liturgy of the Church of England* (2nd edn, London, 1846), p. xcii.

22   That is, 1549.

23   Maskell, *The Ancient Liturgy of the Church of England*, p. xliii.

24   Argued for by William Palmer and others like Darwell Stone later, as the "branch" theory of the Catholic Church, of which the Church of England was one branch through which apostolic succession was preserved. See also, p. 82.

25   See more recently Matthew Cheung Salisbury, *Worship in Medieval England* (Leeds: ARC Humanities Press, 2018), pp. 30–1. Salisbury writes of the belief that "the Church of England, and its liturgy, had an ancient and noble origin equal to and distinct from the Roman Rite as it had developed in continental Europe. This of course is not true, and Bishop knew it." This is certainly what Maskell believed, and he was perhaps not as categorically wrong as Bishop (and Salisbury) affirm. See also p. 84, Note 18.

26 Maskell, *The Ancient Liturgy of the Church of England*, (3rd edn, Oxford: Clarendon Press, 1882), pp. xxiii–xxiv.

27 Ibid., pp. lxxxiii–lxxxiv.

28 Dearmer begins his Introduction to *The Parson's Handbook* in typically uncompromising form, reviewing "the lamentable confusion, lawlessness, and vulgarity which are conspicuous in the Church at this time. The confusion is due to the want of liturgical knowledge among the clergy, and of consistent example among those in authority" (new edn, London: Grant Richards, 1903), p. 1.

29 See, Matthew Cheung Salisbury, "Rethinking the Uses of Sarum and York: A Historiographical Essay", in Helen Gittos and Sarah Hamilton (eds), *Understanding Medieval Liturgy: Essays in Interpretation* (London: Routledge, 2016), pp. 105–6. See also p. 36.

30 Maskell, *Monumenta Ritualia Ecclesiae Anglicanae*, Vol. 1 (2nd edn, Oxford: Clarendon Press, 1882), pp. ix–x.

31 See Chapter 16.

32 See for example his discussion of the early Prymers in his "Dissertation on Service Books" in *Monumenta Ritualia*, Vol. 1, 2nd edn, p. clxxxiii.

33 T. F. Simmons (ed.), *The Lay Folks' Mass Book*, Ed. EETS OS 71 (London: N. Trübner, 1879), p. 231.

1 3

Francis Procter, *A History of the Book of Common Prayer* (1855)

Francis Procter's long life can hardly be described as eventful, though his name holds an important position in the history of the Book of Common Prayer. He was born on 21 June 1812 in London, of modest background—his father was a warehouseman—but at the same time with good family connections. His early years were spent with his uncle Payler Procter, a clergyman in Newland, Gloucestershire and at Shrewsbury School where the headmaster was Samuel Butler (1774–1839), the future Bishop of Lichfield and grandfather of the celebrated writer Samuel Butler.[1] The world of educated people in Victorian England was a small one indeed.

In 1831, Procter matriculated at St Catharine's College, Cambridge. Another uncle, Joseph Procter, was Master of the college. Graduating in 1835, he was ordained deacon in the Diocese of Lincoln in 1836, and then ordained priest in the Diocese of Ely in 1838. A man of studious inclination, he served two curacies before returning to Cambridge in 1842 as fellow and tutor at his old college. What was to prove his last move was in 1847 when, at the age of 35, he accepted the parish of Witton in Norfolk, where he remained for 58 years until his death on 24 August 1905 at the age of 93. In those days, incumbents having a freehold in their parish were frequently not in a position to retire, having no other source of income apart from their stipend and no other home apart from their rectory or vicarage. Procter married Margaret Meryon in 1848, with whom he had eight children. Procter's long and largely secluded life thus spanned almost the entire nineteenth century.

As was the case with many other clergymen, and is perhaps right, little is recorded of Procter's pastoral and parochial ministry, but

106

he is best known today for one great work, his *History of the Book of Common Prayer, with a Rationale of its Offices* (1855). A second edition appeared in the following year with five reprints before a third edition was published in 1870. There were no less than 11 further reprints with additional material being added in 1880 and 1889. Finally, four years before Procter's death and with his full approval, the book was extensively revised and enlarged by the eminent liturgist Walter Howard Frere, of the Community of the Resurrection, Mirfield, in 1901, and it continued to be published with various further additions and corrections throughout much of the twentieth century. In many respects, it was only finally replaced by Geoffrey Cuming's *A History of Anglican Liturgy* (1969; second edition, 1982), yet it remains valuable even today, affectionately known as simply "Procter and Frere".

Before turning in more detail to Procter's *History of the Book of Common Prayer*, which in some respects can be regarded as a textbook written for his "students" (a word he often uses), who were actually Procter's fellow clergy, his less well known and later writings should not be entirely neglected. These books clearly establish him as a scholar of considerable learning, giving further attention to the medieval origins of the liturgy of the Prayer Book and emphasizing the liturgical independence of the English Church from Rome, despite its foundations from Rome through St Augustine of Canterbury.[2] Sent as a missionary by Pope Gregory the Great, Augustine, Procter affirms, "arrived, doubtless bringing with him the Ritual that was at that time used in Rome".[3] At the same time, having become acquainted with the "Gallican Use" in his travels to Britain, Augustine

> introduced into England a form of Liturgy founded on the Roman model, with ordinary Daily Offices derived from the southern French churches,[4] thus giving to the English Church its own national Use. Certain it is that the entire Roman Ritual was never used, although attempts were made to force it upon the Anglo-Saxon Church.[5]

This claim for English medieval liturgical independence from Rome drew Procter to the further study of medieval liturgy, beginning with the Sarum Breviary. His edition of the Breviary, made with Christopher Wordsworth[6] as joint editor, drew upon Procter's own transcription of the text printed in Paris in 1531,[7] and he described the Sarum Breviary as "most remarkable . . . a reformation of the Ritual based on earlier English and Norman customs".[8] This work in three volumes was finally published in its complete form in 1886, and is described in Procter's ODNB entry, written by Frere,[9] as "the most notable achievement of an era which was first developing the systematic study of medieval service books". In 1893 (at the age of 81), Procter again collaborated with Christopher Wordsworth and others in the publication of *The Martiloge in Englysshe after the Use of the Chirche of Salisbury and as it is redde in Syon with Addicyons*. This was an edition of a martyrology printed by Wynkyn de Worde in 1526.

Apart from his major liturgical work on the Prayer Book and pre-Reformation liturgical texts, Procter published a number of other smaller works, including a shorter history of the Prayer Book: *Christ and Other Masters: An Historical Enquiry into some of the chief parallelisms and contrasts between Christianity and the Religious Systems of the Ancient World* (1874, reprinted 1875, 1882, 1886); *Classified Gems of Thought from the Great Writers and Preachers of all Ages* (1892); *An Elementary History of the Book of Common Prayer* (1866); and, *A History of the Articles of Religion: to which is added a series of documents from A. D. 1236 to A. D. 1615* (1876, reprinted 1884).

Procter was one of the first members of the secular Early English Text Society,[10] along with many other scholarly Anglican parish priests. Although he was a lifelong pastor in rural Norfolk whose scholarly work cannot be separated from his parochial vocation, his work was a significant part of the further shift of liturgical study to a largely historical and even technical (rather than pastoral) exercise that eventually tended to lose its practical roots in the tradition of Anglican Prayer Book commentaries that we have been following. Such a shift would have its consequences in the more academically professionalized world of the twentieth century.

Nevertheless, Procter firmly situates his great *History of the Book of Common Prayer* in the tradition of Anglican commentary that reaches back, in Procter's case quite critically, to Sparrow and L'Estrange in the seventeenth century and reached its peak in Wheatly's *Rational*

Illustration of the Book of Common Prayer in the early eighteenth century.[11] He writes that "it was mainly with the view of epitomizing their extensive publications, and correcting by their help sundry traditional errors, or misconceptions, that the present volume was put together".[12] Within the great tradition of Prayer Book studies, Procter also saw himself as its corrective. Specifically in his Preface, he cites the work of John Strype (1643–1737),[13] William Nicholls (*A Comment on the Book of Common Prayer*, 1710), Thomas Comber (*A Companion to the Temple*, 1672-6) and Wheatly. He deliberately and significantly does not include Bishop Sparrow's *Rationale upon the Book of Common Prayer* (1655) "from the feeling that that excellent little volume will be in the hands of every student".[14] Here he may have been a little too optimistic about the reading habits of his fellow parish clergy. Procter then cites more recent studies from the nineteenth century including the work of Edward Cardwell, William Palmer, William Maskell, William Keatinge Clay,[15] Thomas Lathbury[16] and John Henry Blunt.[17] Procter's *History of the Book of Common Prayer* was originally dedicated to the memory of John James Blunt, Lady Margaret professor of divinity in Cambridge from 1838, who died in the year of the book's first publication.

Procter's historical learning is considerable, his theology at best cautious. A product of the University of Cambridge, he does not, like many if not most other High Church Anglican liturgical scholars of his time, look back to the Oxford Movement, the Tractarians and their preoccupations. In true Anglican spirit, he is careful not to be too precise in his definition of a sacrament—in a broader definition, for Procter, this would include confirmation, but in the narrower there are only the two scriptural sacraments acknowledged in the catechism—baptism and the Eucharist. His description of the Consecration in the Prayer Book service of Holy Communion is nothing if not reticent:

> It is carefully worded, to exclude all notions of any physical change in the material elements, by virtue of which they are identified or confounded with the Body and Blood of Christ: but we pray that we may so receive those creatures of God, as to partake of that Body and Blood, truly and really,[18] in a sacramental manner, according to the full meaning of Christ's ordinance, *whatever that*

may be, without specifying the hidden way in which the earthly elements are made conductors of the heavenly grace.[19]

In a Church of England that was still emerging from the furore of the Gorham Case of 1847 (which, as discussed in Chapter 12, saw a number of Anglican clergy, Maskell among them, secede to Rome), it was wise not to be disputatious with regard to the theology of baptism. Procter, drawing directly on Archbishop Cranmer (*Reformatio Legum ecclesiasticarum*, "de baptismo") merely "acknowledges the certain regeneration of every Infant in Baptism, but attributes all to the Divine promise, not to any virtue residing in the element".[20] Frere adds very little to this in his revisions, but he does, at times make significant additions to Procter, as, for example, in his rather prim "correction"[21] of Procter's bland description of confirmation. Procter simply writes:

> Confirmation occupies an important position in the economy of the Church, which is pointed out in the last rubric,[22] that it is the admission to full communion.[23]

Frere's significant expansion of this, emphasizing the gift of the Holy Spirit in confirmation, reads:

> Beyond its own intrinsic importance, as the gift of the Spirit and the corollary of Baptism, confirmation occupies further an important position in the economy of the Church, which is pointed out in the last rubric, in that it is the admission to full communion: for it is only natural that the reception of the fulness [sic] of the gift of the Spirit offered to every member of Christ should be first required of those who come to the Lord's Supper.[24]

A comparison between Procter's original work and the extensive revisions and additions by Frere (all made entirely with Procter's blessing) throws some significant light on the development of Anglican liturgical scholarship in the second half of the nineteenth century. To start with, Procter was still of the generation of scholar parish priests who combined faithful pastoral ministry with serious scholarship and saw no conflict between them. This generation included men such as Thomas Frederick Simmons or John Christopher Atkinson of Yarm, North Yorkshire, both of whom, like Procter, though less well remembered today, produced significant scholarly work in various fields.[25] For them, the parochial vocation and serious scholarship fed into one another. Frere, on the other hand, although not a professional university academic in the modern sense of the word, lived much of his life within the context of the Community of the Resurrection, Mirfield, though he was, for a while, the Bishop of Truro (1923–35). Second, although both Frere and Procter were Cambridge graduates, Frere imbibed the spirit of the Tractarian tradition to a much greater extent in his theology and liturgy. Finally, and ultimately perhaps of most importance, if Procter looks back to the post-Reformation, and essentially pastoral, tradition within the Church of the commentaries on the Prayer Book from Sparrow to Wheatly, Frere lays much greater emphasis on the medieval origins of the Prayer Book and its liturgy, and this is reflected in his revisions of Procter's book.

Phillip Tovey has rightly stated that Procter does not directly look back to the bookish layman Hamon L'Estrange and his *Alliance of Divine Offices* (1659), with its carefully aligned parallel texts that look forward to such works as that of William Maskell or, later, the deeply scholarly *The English Rite* (1915) of F. E. Brightman, or even more recently Peter Jagger's *Christian Initiation, 1552–1969* (1970).[26] Rather Procter's book sits more comfortably within the learned clerical and pastoral tradition of the commentaries of Sparrow, Wheatly and even perhaps Bishop Thomas Wilson and his *Short and Plain Instruction for the Understanding of the Lord's Supper* (1733).

When it comes to Frere, to whom we shall devote a chapter later in this book (17), however, not only does he considerably expand Procter's work—Frere's revision is about half as long again as the original book—he adds three chapters to the history of the Prayer Book (Part 1), not least vastly expanding the discussion of the pre-Reformation period. Frere, and indeed to some extent Procter himself, were part of the veritable industry of scholarship on medieval liturgical texts in England in the later years of the nineteenth century. This industry was spurred on originally by the fathers of the Oxford Movement in their ecclesiological concern to establish the historical continuity through the millennia of the "English

Church", and was promoted further as antiquarian interests became more serious and learned in secular societies like the Early English Text Society (a substantial percentage of whose early members and contributors were clergy) and the more overtly religious Henry Bradshaw Society, which was founded in 1890 to promote through publication the study of medieval and early modern liturgies.[27] At the end of Part 1 in his revised book, Frere adds the full texts, in Greek and Latin, of ancient and medieval liturgies, including texts from the Liturgy of St Chrysostom and the Sarum Use.[28] Frere also extends Procter's history of the Prayer Book, which effectively ends with the reign of Charles II (with a brief appendix on the eighteenth century) up to the end of the nineteenth century and the publication of the experimental and never approved *Convocation Prayer Book* of 1880.[29] He also says a great deal more about the Scottish Prayer Book of 1637, which probably had more effect on the Prayer Book of 1662 in England than it ever did in Scotland, and then its subsequent effect in the development of the Episcopal Church in the United States of America.[30]

And so, although their names are bound together in the collective memory as "Procter and Frere", a name by which their book has been known to generations of Anglican ordinands and clergy, the two men were very different in a number of important ways. Procter was liturgically conservative, unwilling to disturb the treasure that was the Book of Common Prayer and equally unwilling to engage in theological debates. He would essentially have agreed with William van Mildert, the future Bishop of Durham, on the importance for the Church of England of maintaining the beauty and integrity of the BCP. He was certainly not a revisionist, unlike Frere. Francis Procter has almost been forgotten as a parish priest serving for more than 50 years in Witton, Norfolk. This silence reflects little upon his incumbency beyond the fact that few records survive—as is also the case with Thomas Frederick Simmons in Yorkshire and many others. Such men served the Church and their people quietly and without public ambition. Frere's brief ODNB entry for Procter has few sources to draw upon beyond his publications together with information provided by his daughter in 1912, the records of his school in Shrewsbury, St Catharine's College, Cambridge, the Clergy List (1904) and *Crockford's Clerical Directory*. Walter Howard Frere, by contrast, and despite his monastic vocation in Mirfield, was very much a public figure, well known nationally and indeed internationally. He was also aware of the need for the Church of England to reform its Prayer Book, inspired by earlier Tractarians and such churchmen as J. M. Neale, who recognized that the pastoral needs of the Church of England in the nineteenth century required, in Neale's words, "the revision, or rather enlargement of the Prayer-book [as] a work which cannot be much longer delayed".[31]

Yet together "Procter and Frere" remains a landmark in Prayer Book scholarship and commentary, standing between two ages in the history of Anglican liturgy. Francis Procter stood at the end of a long tradition of Anglican liturgical scholarship dating back to the mid-seventeenth century. Its focus was ultimately pastoral, reviewing the Book of Common Prayer in its various forms from 1549, and its historical roots in the early Church and through the "Gallican" tradition in English worship in the Middle Ages up to the Reformation. Though in some ways now dated and even highly questionable, this was scholarship with an ecclesiological purpose—to sustain a vision of the Church of England as truly ancient and universal, with the Reformation regarded as an exercise in revision and repair rather than revolution. Procter, like many other Church of England clergymen with a scholarly inclination, was also and essentially a parish priest, his life almost hidden in the rural village of Norfolk which he served for so long. Frere's life as a monk of Mirfield and Bishop of Truro, on the other hand, was on a much more public platform, involved too with matters of Church and State, not least in the Prayer Book controversy of 1927/1928 as well as ecumenical negotiations with Rome in the Malines Conversations. In the twentieth century, liturgical scholarship largely, if not entirely, lost its roots in the common life of the Church of England—the true place for the use and study of the Book of Common Prayer—as parish priests, by and large, were drawn away from serious scholarship. Meanwhile, the academic world became the professional centre for such work, and liturgical study became a matter of revision in the global context of ecumenism alongside an anxious Church that was rapidly losing its central place within the national culture of England. Parishes were now "consulted" on the proposed revisions of liturgy committees rather than being educated by liturgically well-informed parochial clergy.

Perhaps as liturgical debate became more cultural rather than historical and theological, and the Book of Common Prayer became a volume of historical interest rather than of communal devotional vibrancy—so the study of liturgy as known by Francis Procter began to fade away and lose its true sense of vocation and community.

Notes

[1] Best known for his utopian novel *Erewhon* (1872) and autobiographical novel *The Way of All Flesh* (1903).

[2] Procter's lengthy reference to the mission of St Augustine is omitted by Frere in his revisions of Procter's work.

[3] Francis Procter, *A History of the Book of Common Prayer* (16th edn, London: Macmillan, 1881), p. 2.

[4] These, Procter notes, may have ultimately derived from Eastern sources through Cassian. See also, Philip Freeman, *The Principles of Divine Service: An Enquiry Concerning the True Manner of Understanding and Using the Order for Morning and Evening Prayer, and for the Administration of the Holy Communion in the English Church* (Oxford: John Henry & James Parker, 1862), Vol. 1, pp. 249ff.

[5] Procter, *A History of the Book of Common Prayer*, p. 3. See further, W. S. Porter, *The Gallican Rite*, The Alcuin Club (London: A. R. Mowbray, 1958).

[6] Christopher Wordsworth (1848–1938) is not to be confused with his father, Bishop Christopher Wordsworth. The younger man was a parish priest, liturgical scholar and chancellor of both Lincoln and Salisbury Cathedrals. Among his many liturgical works are *Notes on Medieval Services in England* (1898) and (with Henry Littlehales) *The Old Service-Books of the English Church* (1904).

[7] Further assistance was given by Henry Bradshaw and others.

[8] Quoted in Phillip Tovey, "Francis Procter", in Christopher Irvine (ed.), *They Shaped Our Worship: Essays on Anglican Liturgists*, Alcuin Club Collections 75 (London: SPCK, 1998), p. 12.

[9] Now revised by H. C. G. Matthew.

10 The EETS was founded in 1864 as a "club" by F. J. Furnivall, partly to provide resources for what was later to become the Oxford English Dictionary.

11 Procter specifically refers to the "best edition" of Wheatly, with additional notes by G. E. Corrie, published by Cambridge University Press in 1858. Preface to *A History of the Book of Common Prayer*, p. v.

12 Procter, *A History of the Book of Common Prayer*, p. v.

13 Strype's extensive writings on the Reformation Church of England were reprinted in 59 volumes in Oxford between 1812 and 1824.

14 Procter, *A History of the Book of Common Prayer*, p. vi.

15 W. K. Clay, *The Book of Common Prayer Illustrated So as to Show its Various Modifications, the Date of its Several Parts, and the Authority on Which they Rest* (London, 1841); (ed.), *Liturgies and Occasional Forms of Prayer Set Forth in the Reign of Queen Elizabeth*, Parker Society (Cambridge University Press, 1847); *An Historical Sketch of the Prayer Book* (1849).

16 Thomas Lathbury, *A History of the Convocation of the Church of England* (London, 1842).

17 J. H. Blunt, *The Annotated Book of Common Prayer* (1884). He is not to be confused with Professor John James Blunt. See Chapter 15.

18 The footnote here includes comments from Archbishop Laud and John Calvin.

19 Procter, *A History of the Book of Common Prayer*, p. 357 (emphases added).

20 Ibid., p. 376.

21 Phillip Tovey's word, "Francis Procter", p. 11.

22 Drawn directly from the Sarum Manual.

23 Procter, *A History of the Book of Common Prayer*, p. 405.

24 Francis Procter, revised and rewritten, Walter Howard Frere, *A New History of the Book of Common Prayer* [1905] (London: Macmillan, 1949), pp. 606–7.

25 J. C. Atkinson (1814–1900) contributed significantly to philological studies, writing for the English Dialect Society, while also contributing major works on the history of Whitby and Rievaulx abbeys (for the Surtees Society), as well as being an accomplished ornithologist. His ODNB entry notes that "Atkinson's scholarly activity was an integral part of his Christian ministry".

26 Yet it should be noted that Jagger completed his work when working as a parish priest in Leeds, though he subsequently became Warden and Chief Librarian at St Deiniol's Library, Hawarden.

27 Both of these societies continue to flourish today.

116 THE BOOK OF COMMON PRAYER AND ITS COMMENTATORS

[28] He rearranged some of these from Procter's inclusion of them in Chapter 3 on the order for Holy Communion of Part 2, which Procter entitled "The Sources and Rationale of its (BCP) Offices".

[29] Procter and Frere, *A New History of the Book of Common Prayer*, p. 225.

[30] Ibid., pp. 234–53.

[31] J. M. Neale, *Essays on Liturgiology and Church History* (London: Saunders, Otley & Co., 1863), p. 225.

1 4

John Mason Neale, *Essays on Liturgiology and Church History* (1863)

John Mason Neale was born in London on 24 January 1818 of staunchly evangelical parents. His father, Cornelius Neale, was also a clergyman, though his ordination was rather late in life, and a fellow of St John's College, Cambridge. He was a man of some literary talent and an accomplished poet—traits which his son John inherited. Cornelius Neale died in 1823 and John was brought up by his mother from the age of five. Although he gained a scholarship at Trinity College, Cambridge, he took only an ordinary degree, failing honours, which at that time in Cambridge required success in the Mathematical Tripos, which John found not to his taste. This did not prevent him, however, from being elected as a Fellow tutor of Downing College, and his developing passion for antiquarianism led him towards a high churchmanship that at Cambridge resulted in his establishing, with his friend Benjamin Webb (1819–85), the Cambridge Camden Society—later renamed the Ecclesiological Society—in 1839, whose concerns were with the architecture and decoration of churches. It can be seen, in some respects, as the Cambridge equivalent of the Oxford Movement, leading the way in the Church of England to the revival of a "medieval" kind of architecture (the so called "English Gothic" style most characteristically represented in the style of Augustus Pugin and his followers), together with the use of vestments and ceremonial.

The architectural principles espoused by the Camden Society— aesthetic, liturgical and theological—were embodied in a work by Neale and Webb of 1843 entitled *The Symbolism of Churches and Church Ornaments*. This, with its lengthy Introductory Essay, was in fact a translation of the first book of Bishop William Durandus' *Rationale*

Divinorum Officiorum, and of it James F. White, an historian of the "Cambridge Movement", has suggested that "it is difficult to overestimate the importance of this work for it materially changed the course of ecclesiology".[1] Originally written between 1286 and 1295, Bishop Durandus' work is arguably the most important medieval Latin treatise on the symbolism of church architecture and the rituals of worship, and Neale and Webb's lengthy introductory essay entitled "Sacramentality: A Principle of Ecclesiastical Design" established Neale in his enduring love for the Middle Ages and medieval liturgy, with its profound influence on the Victorian Church of England and its development of worship as rooted in the Book of Common Prayer.[2]

Neale and Webb's *Durandus* was published one year after Neale's ordination to the Anglican priesthood in 1842, the year also of his marriage to Sarah Norman Webster. The offer of the parish of Crawley in Sussex was never taken up, as persistent ill health—he was diagnosed with consumption—took Neale to the milder climate of Madeira, where he largely remained until the summer of 1844. Improved health in Madeira led to an enormous outpouring of writings, among them his series of distinctly quaint novels descriptive of English Church history, including *Ayton Priory* (1843) and *Shepperton Manor* (1843).[3] The latter sets out to portray the English Church at the beginning of the seventeenth century, "its internal discipline and ceremonies", and contains a portrait of Bishop Lancelot Andrewes, whose writings Neale was at the time translating into Portuguese.[4] But most important by far of his Madeira writings was the first volume of *The History of the Holy Eastern Church*, a work finally completed in 1873 in three volumes by George Williams after Neale's death. Encouraged by no less than Edward Bouverie Pusey and William Palmer of Magdalen College, Oxford, Neale immersed himself in the history and liturgy of the Eastern Church as maintaining, for him, the purest links with the early Church, untainted by the Reformation or papal dominance. Much later, in 1859, with his close friend R. F. Littledale,[5] Neale also translated and edited *The Liturgies of SS. Mark, James, Clement, Chrysostom, and Basil, and the Church of Malabar* (1859). Neale noted in his Preface that "it has for many years been my desire to render these most pure sources of Eucharistic Doctrine accessible to all my brethren", citing as a further authority in English the work of William Palmer of Worcester College, Oxford in his *Origines Liturgicae*.[6]

In 1846, Neale was back in England and appointed to the wardenship of Sackville College, East Grinstead, a small establishment founded for the care of a few pensioners and with a modest stipend of £28 a year.[7] Here, in 1854, Neale established the sisterhood which survives today as the Society of Margaret, initially offering nursing care to the poor of the neighbourhood. Neale's ministry was not without its opposition. In 1847, the Bishop of Chichester, Ashurst Gilbert Turner, inhibited Neale from sacramental and clerical functions because of the bishop's fear of Neale's admittedly extreme High Church practices. The inhibition was not formally lifted until 1863. Then, in 1857, there were riots in the town of Lewes, East Sussex, where the rural dean, John Scobell, accused Neale of tempting his daughter Emily into the sisterhood in order to gain access to her wealth. This was certainly not the case. The issue blew over and the sisterhood flourished. Neale remained in East Grinstead for the rest of his life, refusing a far more lucrative offer of preferment in the Scottish Episcopal Church.[8]

Neale's professional life in the Church of England, then, was humble, but his enduring influence on the Church was remarkable as a result not only of his liturgical scholarship but also, and perhaps above all, his hymn writing and translation of ancient and medieval Latin canticles and hymns. In 1863, Neale published a volume entitled *Essays on Liturgiology and Church History*. It was here that he most forcefully expressed his belief in the need for the revision and expansion of the Book of Common Prayer in the interest of the expanding pastoral needs of the Church. Quite simply, the Prayer Book of the Victorian Church, essentially unrevised for some 200 years since 1662, was not fit for the growing requirements of the nineteenth-century Church of England. Neale wrote in a manner that begs translation into more contemporary terms today in the matter of liturgical revision and renewal:

> The revision, or rather enlargement of the Prayer-book, is a work which cannot be much longer delayed. When once the subject is brought before English Churchmen, they will feel that the cautious conservatism of merely working up old materials into

120   THE BOOK OF COMMON PRAYER AND ITS COMMENTATORS

> new services, is one which can satisfy nobody and will equally offend those who would be offended by any change. We *must* have a new Evening Service. We *must* have an authorized Office for the Consecration of Churches and Churchyards. We *must* have a greater variety of Collects for the great variety of temporal wants; for example, those of travellers, and for the infinite number of spiritual necessities unmentioned in the Prayer-book.[9]

The nineteenth century saw a shift in the Church of England from a general satisfaction with the Book of Common Prayer to a growing sense of its inadequacy to meet the spiritual, pastoral and cultural demands of a changing Church.[10] Neale was acutely conscious of this need for quite radical revision and change, his proposals looking forward to revisions of the Prayer Book that would only be realized, in part, in the twentieth century. In a broader sphere, Neale was, in addition, influenced by the philological writings of Archbishop Richard Chenevix Trench (1807–86) and such works as *On the Study of Words* (1851), which was influential for the early work on the *Oxford English Dictionary*[11] and the scholarly editorial work of such organizations as the Early English Text Society. In the nineteenth century, the study of liturgy was far from being a culturally isolated exercise.

But alongside his work on Eastern liturgies and the Book of Common Prayer, it was as a hymnwriter and translator that Neale was known and is primarily remembered today, his entry meriting no less than 11 columns in John Julian's magisterial *A Dictionary of Hymnology* (1892). It was work which he saw as complementary to his concerns for the BCP. Neale followed such nineteenth-century hymnwriters as John Keble and Richard Mant[12] in drawing deeply on early and medieval hymns as well as the ancient hymns of the Eastern Church. Neale's first publications in this field were *Hymns for Children* (1842) and *Hymns for the Sick* (1843), linking the sick person with the suffering Christ and indicative already of the close link in Neale between the hymn, the Prayer Book and sound Christian doctrine. Later collections include *Mediaeval Hymns and Sequences* (1851) and *Hymns, Chiefly Mediaeval, on the Joys and Glories of Paradise* (1865). In his summary of Neale's hymns, J. R. Watson has proposed that "Neale was engaged in a massive and innovative project, an attempt to swing the writing and appreciation of hymns away from a post-Reformation individualism into a nobler and deeper impersonality".[13] It was a noble and catholic vision, and Neale shared with the Tractarians a strong sense of the principle of reserve in matters of religion and a dislike of evangelical subjectivity and sentimentalism. From his two collections of carols (1853 and 1854, for Christmas and Easter respectively), by far his most familiar carol is "Good King Wenceslas", taken from a prose tale in his own rather Dickensian book of children's stories, *Deeds of Faith* (1849).

Today Neale's hymns survive largely through the medium of that enduring Anglican hymnbook, *Hymns Ancient & Modern*. First published in 1861 under the editorship of H. W. Baker (1821–77), *Hymns A&M* was a product of the Oxford Movement and deliberately designed to be used alongside the liturgy of the Book of Common Prayer, drawing largely on medieval and modern sources, with many of the traditional Office hymns being the work of Neale.[14] They include hymns for the third, sixth and ninth canonical hours, translations from St Ambrose, the Latin evening hymn *O Lux Beata*, and the evening hymn "The day is past and over", translated from the Greek of probably the sixth-century Anatolius (*Τὴν ἡμέραν διελθών*).

Of the nearly 60 of his hymns which remain in the 1950 revision of *Hymns A&M*, some 46 are translations from ancient originals and include "Jerusalem the golden" (a translation of Bernard of Cluny's *Urbs Sion aurea*), "Light's abode, celestial Salem" (a translation of *Jerusalem luminosa*, ascribed to Thomas à Kempis), and "A great and mighty wonder" (translated from the Greek of St Germanus). All remain familiar in Anglican worship today. Sung alongside the public worship of the Book of Common Prayer, Neale's hymns vividly link the contemporary worship of the "catholic and apostolic" Anglican Church with the liturgies of the early Church, the Eastern Church and medieval Christendom.

Neale's concern for the living and ancient tradition of the worship of the Church of England as rooted in the Prayer Book was born of a considerable, and ecumenical, liturgical scholarship that embraced within the liturgy of the Church not simply texts but church architecture and furnishings, and a sense of liturgical drama as well as the participation of parochial congregations in the liturgy through the singing of hymns

122 THE BOOK OF COMMON PRAYER AND ITS COMMENTATORS

that were both ancient and modern, and were theologically articulate without being sentimental.

In the American Book of Common Prayer and the Church of England's Lectionary for Common Worship, Neale is remembered on 7 August as "John Mason Neale, Priest and Hymn Writer". Neale died, aged only 48 and after a series of operations, on the feast of the Transfiguration, 6 August 1866. He is buried in the churchyard in East Grinstead. No church dignitaries were in attendance at his funeral.

Notes

[1] James F. White, *The Cambridge Movement: The Ecclesiologists and the Gothic Revival* (Cambridge: Cambridge University Press, 1962), p. 68.

[2] See also p. 7 on Anthony Sparrow's use of the title of Durandus' work for his own commentary on the BCP.

[3] See in more detail Eleanor A. Towle, *John Mason Neale D.D. A Memoir* (London: Longmans, Green & Co., 1906), p. 83. At one point during his time in Madeira, Neale was writing his novels at a rate of one every three weeks. SPCK continued to print Neale's novels into the twentieth century "to meet a continuous demand for his work".

[4] J. M. Neale, *Shepperton Manor* [1843] (London: SPCK, 1909), pp. v–viii. Part of Neale's childhood was spent at Shepperton in north Surrey.

[5] Richard Frederick Littledale (1833–90) was a clergyman who, like Neale, suffered from ill health which prevented him from undertaking parochial duties after 1861. He contributed to a number of works on practical principles of Anglo-Catholic worship including *The Priest's Prayer Book* (1864) and *The Altar Manual* (1863). Littledale completed Neale's unfinished *Commentary on the Psalms from Primitive and Medieval Writers* (1868).

[6] J. M. Neale and R. F. Littledale, *The Liturgies of SS. Mark, James, Clement, Chrysostom, and Basil* (7th edn, London: Griffith Farran & Co., 1869), p. vii.

[7] It was more than reminiscent of Hiram's Hospital in Trollope's novel *The Warden* (1855).

[8] In 1850, Neale was offered the relatively well-endowed post of provost of St Ninian's Cathedral in Perth, Scotland. Despite a lifelong interest in the

Scottish Episcopal Church, Neale declined the offer, fearing the effect of the harsher climate of Scotland on his weak health.

9 J. M. Neale, *Essays on Liturgiology and Church History* (London: Saunders, Otley & Co., 1863), p. 225. Travel, of course, was becoming much more commonplace in the second half of the nineteenth century, with the rapid development of railways and steamships.

10 See Bryan Spinks, "The Transition from 'Excellent Liturgy' to being 'Too Narrow for the Religious Life of the Present Generation': The Book of Common Prayer in the Nineteenth Century", in Stephen Platten and Christopher Woods (eds), *Comfortable Words: Polity, Piety and the Book of Common Prayer* (London: SCM Press, 2012), pp. 98–120.

11 Trench was Archbishop of Dublin from 1864–84. His vision for the OED was of a "*lexicon totius Anglicitatis*"—an "entirely new Dictionary; no patch upon old garments, but a new garment throughout".

12 On Mant as hymnwriter see p. 61.

13 J. R. Watson, *The English Hymn: A Critical and Historical Study* (Oxford: Oxford University Press, 2004), p. 379.

14 Among the many subsequent editions of *Hymns A&M*, *An Historical Edition of Hymns Ancient and Modern* was edited by Bishop Walter Frere and published in 1909.

1 5

John Henry Blunt, *The Annotated Book of Common Prayer* (1866)

John Henry Blunt was born on 25 August 1823 in Chelsea, where his father, Robert Blunt, was a chemist. After attending a private school in Chelsea, Blunt followed his father's profession as a chemist for some time, marrying Frances Ousby (1816–94), the daughter of a clergyman, in Holy Trinity, Chelsea.

Then, at the age of 27, Blunt became a student of University College in the new University of Durham, being ordained deacon in 1852 and priest in 1855, when he was also awarded his MA by his university. After curacies in Northumberland and Hampshire, Blunt was appointed vicar of Kennington, Oxfordshire in 1868, and in 1873 he was given the crown living of Beverston in Gloucestershire, where he remained until his death in 1884, caused possibly through overwork, aged 61. He became a Doctor of Divinity of the University of Durham in 1882.[1]

Blunt was an energetic author, widely known in the Church of England for his writings in reviews and church journals, publishing his first book, *Atonement*, in 1855, while still a curate. He published a standard work on canon law, *The Book of Church Law*, in 1872, but he was best known for his work in the two connected fields of pastoral theology and liturgy. Blunt's handbook for the parish priest, the *Directorium Pastorale*, was published in 1864 and regularly reprinted for much of the nineteenth century. It reflects his High Church views on the theology and practice of the Church of England, impressing upon parish clergy the need for spiritual discipline, not least in the regular saying of Morning and Evening Prayer on a daily basis, and most properly in churches that should all be "open daily for public prayer throughout England".[2] Blunt's

Directorium became a standard work for parish priests, his High Church principles applied with considerable pastoral sensitivity, and with a clear sense of the state of society at the time. For example, he advocated private confession as a potentially creative way of fostering proper relationships between priests and their people, noting that "many holy, far-sighted and experienced clergymen look upon [confession] as a valuable part of the pastor's work".[3] But he also stressed the absolute seal of the confessional and the silence enjoined upon clergy on hearing any "communications . . . not manifestly of an open kind". In the practical social sphere, the *Directorium* provides parish priests with detailed information on the setting up of penny banks to encourage regular saving among the poor, and links them with clothing and coal clubs. He refers his reader to the writings of the Revd J. Erskine Clarke, vicar of St Michael's, Derby, who was secretary of the Derby Working Men's Association Penny Bank.[4] Blunt's concern for the liturgy and public worship of the Church was far from being abstracted from the daily, practical needs of parishioners, often in the poorest parts of society.

Blunt's most enduring work is his meticulously written and edited *Annotated Book of Common Prayer, being, An Historical, Ritual, and Theological Commentary on the Devotional System of the Church of England* (1866), which was regularly reprinted and, in the words of his biographer in the ODNB, T. F. Tout, even today "is still of some value".[5] Blunt wrote by far the greatest part of the book and its lengthy annotations to the 1662 Prayer Book, but as its editor he also drew upon the labours of a distinguished group of contemporaries, including William Bright (1824–1901) who, after a period as a parish priest, became regius professor of Ecclesiastical History at Oxford in 1868, and was known for his historical work on liturgy, particularly his book *Ancient Collects and Other Prayers* (1857). In the central essays and annotations on the "Order for the Holy Communion" in the *Annotated Book of Common Prayer*, Blunt collaborated with Peter G. Medd (1829–1908), a cleric who was known for his work on Bishop Lancelot Andrewes, but more especially his widely used (and anonymously published) manual for clergy, *The Priest to the Altar, or, Aids to the Devout Celebration of Holy Communion, chiefly after the Ancient English Use of Sarum* (1861).[6] *The Priest to the Altar*, like Blunt's *Annotated Prayer Book*, prints a full text of the 1637 Scottish Communion office. Other contributors to the *Annotated Prayer Book* include the rector of St Oswald's, Durham and notable church musician John Bacchus Dykes, and Thomas Walter Perry, vicar of St Mary the Virgin, Ardleigh, Essex and a member of the Royal Commission on Ritual, 1867–70.[7]

It is clear from the outset that Blunt's primary concern in the *Annotated Prayer Book* is to emphasize, as so often before in the history of Prayer Book commentaries, the ancient patristic and medieval origins of the BCP and to play down the Reformation as the origin and beginning of Cranmer's 1549 Book of Common Prayer and its successors. After providing a formidable list of the "principal Liturgical and Historical authorities" which are used in his book, beginning alphabetically with Amalarius of Metz (*c.*780–850),[8] Blunt first seeks to establish the origins of the "formularies" of "the Church of England",[9] writing: "The earliest history of these formularies is obscure, but there is good reason to believe that they were derived through Lyons, from the great patriarchate of Ephesus, in which St John spent the latter half of his life."[10] Blunt is keen, like so many in the nineteenth century, to stress the "Gallican" ancestry of the English liturgy, "differing in many particulars from [that] of Rome". In short, the Prayer Book is both catholic and ancient, yet not "Roman". On the other hand, Blunt writes consistently and with unbridled and vehement negativity about the "Puritans" and the "Presbyterians". The communion liturgy of the Directory of 1644, from the Commonwealth period, for example, he describes as a "presumptuous and irreverent parody of the Liturgy", which is only "reluctantly printed for the sake of historical completeness".[11] Sometimes, it seems, the demands of proper scholarship come at a price.

In his Preface, Blunt refers first to the work of three prominent nineteenth-century liturgical scholars, William Palmer, William Maskell and Philip Freeman.[12] References to the work of both Palmer and Maskell are to be found liberally scattered throughout the *Annotated Prayer Book*. But he also draws heavily on the tradition of Anglican writing on the Prayer Book since the seventeenth century, noting in his Preface the by now familiar work of Andrewes, Laud, L'Estrange, Sparrow, Cosin and Elborow.[13] Bishop Cosin, "being thoroughly familiar with the Sarum Missal", and the *Durham Book* of 1661, a draft for the revision of the

Prayer Book in 1661, are possibly his most frequently quoted sources, but he is less persuaded by the works of Comber, Wheatly and Shepherd,[14] which are, he writes, "doubtless of great value in their way", but by placing too much emphasis on the Reformation, "tended in reality to alienate the minds of their readers from all thought of Unity and Fellowship with the Church of our Fathers".[15]

Blunt is consistently concerned "to exhibit more concisely and perspicuously the connexion [sic] between the ancient and modern devotional systems of the Church of England".[16] A careful textual scholar, he uses the text of the so-called Sealed Books of Common Prayer, one of a small number of copies of the BCP printed in 1662 and certified by the Commissioners, sealed with the Great Seal of England to be authoritative in case of any disputes over the authorized wording.[17] Apart from a preponderance of references to the English medieval liturgical tradition and Uses as they were available in the growing number of nineteenth-century critical editions of medieval texts and manuscripts, Blunt frequently and notably refers also to the Jewish origins of the Anglican liturgy.

Not surprisingly by far the greatest attention is given to the text of the Holy Communion, which Blunt annotated together with Medd. They draw extensively on the work of J. M. Neale on the liturgies of the Eastern Church, but primarily their concern is to look back to the Holy Communion text of 1549, which they regard as essentially an abbreviated translation of the Sarum Missal, before the separation of the prayer of consecration from the oblation, which was made in 1552, and which survived into 1662.[18] Blunt and Medd give much emphasis to the theology of "sacrifice" and the Real Presence, but Blunt, rather in the manner of Francis Procter, is too careful a scholar (and perhaps too Anglican in his doctrinal approach) to be drawn into over-precise definitions. He writes:

> Much trouble would have been spared to the Church if there had been less endeavour to define on the one hand what our Lord's words meant, and, on the other, what they do mean. Up to a certain point we can define; beyond a certain point we must be content to leave definition and accept mystery.[19]

Blunt's liturgical scholarship is solid but largely based on the work of others, and it always has a pastoral element and base. His *Annotated Prayer Book* is intended for, and indeed was widely used by, Anglo-Catholic and Tractarian parish clergy earnestly seeking the correct way to conduct public worship within what they believed were the ancient, catholic and apostolic traditions of the English Church. Much attention is given by Blunt and Medd to the matter of ceremonial and the "ritual usages of the Church of England",[20] with careful instructions on vestments, the position of the celebrant at the altar, and the roles of deacons and sub-deacons. All is to be done with decorum, properly and precisely. Holy Communion is to be celebrated at least every Sunday in parish churches and in cathedrals and "wherever reasons of pious expediency make them desirable", on a daily pattern.

In an Appendix to the commentary on Holy Communion, Blunt provides an outline of the Sarum Use, which he simply describes as "the Ancient Liturgy of the Church of England",[21] together with the texts of the Scottish Communion Office of 1764,[22] the liturgy of the American Church, and finally what Blunt calls the "presumptuous and irreverent parody" of the liturgy which is found in the Presbyterian Directory of 1644, during the time of the "persecution of the Church by the Puritans".[23]

Following the controversy surrounding baptismal doctrine during the Gorham case of 1847, Blunt is careful to articulate a robust theology of baptism that acknowledges the "necessity of baptism to salvation" and regeneration.[24] Indeed, overall, avoiding the excesses of what he calls "puritanism" and the "corruption of popery", Blunt offers a comprehensive historical, theological and liturgical guide to the use of the Book of Common Prayer which reflects, to a degree at least, the intellectual capacity and pastoral earnestness of the High Church parish clergy of his day. Arguing in detail for the ritualist reading of the Ornaments Rubric to be found in the Prayer Book before the office of Morning Prayer,[25] Blunt provides a detailed Appendix written by T. F. Perry on "Ecclesiastical Vestments". In short, he offers a far sounder and more balanced guide to Prayer Book worship and ceremonial for Anglo-Catholic clergy than the very widely used and often highly eccentric *Directorium Anglicanum* (1858; revised 1865) by John Purchas and F. G. Lee.[26]

Two years after the publication of the *Annotated Book of Common Prayer*, in 1868, Blunt published a considerably shorter and more accessible book, covering much the same ground without the weight of extensive annotations and historical commentaries, entitled *A Key to the Knowledge and Use of the Book of Common Prayer*. Essentially a distillation of his earlier work, the *Key* is a clear guide to the teaching and use of the Prayer Book. In Chapter 2, entitled "The Prayer Book System of Divine Worship", Blunt carefully articulates that at the heart of all worship is the adoration of God. "Everything that is to be said or done looks towards this purpose."[27] He stresses that worship is an action, not only to be spoken but to be "done", and at its heart is the singing of God's praises. From the Old Testament (in, for example the song of Deborah and Barak [Judges 5], or the Book of Psalms) to the worship of the "Primitive Church", singing is central to the praise of God, as are the voices of the laity. Finally, emphasizing the Petrine doctrine of the priesthood of all believers, Blunt describes "the great share of the Laity in our services".[28] Indeed, he goes on, "the Prayer Book shows . . . that there is almost as much for the lay part of the congregation to say and sing as there is for the Clergy" and "silence for the Laity is wrong". They are the words of a parish priest who is sensible of the needs and contribution to worship of his congregation. Public worship is not just a matter for the clergyman and perhaps a choir speaking and singing "for" the silent people.

Where antiquity cannot be referred to, there is an endearing quality to Blunt's adherence to the "Englishness" of the 1662 Book of Common Prayer (though the Prayer Book of 1549, always and in the end, would have been preferable!), such as in his recommending the use of the Comfortable Words in the service of Holy Communion. Again, his pastoral concerns are foremost.

> It is to quicken the faith of the latter [those who have just been absolved of their sins] in such an absolving Presence of Christ, that the COMFORTABLE WORDS are introduced after the Absolution. They are not found in any other Liturgy, but are dear to the English ear.[29]

This assertion is not, of course, strictly correct, as Cranmer is actually drawing the Comfortable Words from earlier liturgical use in Zwingli and Archbishop Hermann von Wied of Cologne in his *Consultation* of 1547. But the spirit of the comment is certainly true.

Written in the midst of his work as a busy and conscientious parish priest, Blunt's literary output was prodigious, including his *Book of Church Law* (1872), which was long a standard work on the subject. His other writing and editing included a *Dictionary of Doctrinal and Historical Theology* (1870), *A Key to the Knowledge and Use of the Holy Bible* (1873), an *Annotated Bible* in three volumes (1878–9), and a posthumously published *Cyclopedia of Religion* (1884).[30] But of his other work perhaps most characteristic of Blunt's essentially practical and pastoral understanding of ministry rooted in the worship of the Book of Common Prayer is his book published in 1871 and entitled:

> *Household Theology.*
> *A Handbook of Religious Information*
> *Respecting the Holy Bible, the Prayer Book*
> *The Church, the Ministry, Divine Worship*
> *The Creeds, etc, etc.*

It remained in print, and use, for more than three decades, until a new century brought a new era upon the Church of England and its Book of Common Prayer, truly employed at its best and in its time as a book for household theology.

Notes

[1]   He is not to be confused with John James Blunt (to whom Procter dedicated his *History of the Book of Common Prayer*), who after many years as a parish priest in Essex was appointed Lady Margaret professor of divinity in Cambridge in 1839. J. J. Blunt was also known for his work in pastoral theology, principally the posthumously published *Acquirements and Principal Obligations and Duties of the Parish Priest* (1856), drawing upon his pastoral lectures in Cambridge.

JOHN HENRY BLUNT · 131

2 J. H. Blunt, *Directorium Pastorale* (1864), quoted in Brian Heeney, *A Different Kind of Gentleman: Parish Clergy as Professional Men in Early and Mid-Victorian England* (Hamden, CT: Archon Books, 1976), p. 39.

3 Blunt, *Directorium Pastorale*, quoted in Heeney, p. 51.

4 See Heeney, *A Different Kind of Gentleman*, pp. 74–5.

5 The ODNB article was revised by H. C. G. Matthew (2004).

6 My own copy is of the revised and enlarged third edition, published in 1879 and produced as an altar book to be used by the priest in the celebration of Holy Communion.

7 For the work of the Royal Commission see further, R. C. D. Jasper, *Prayer Book Revision in England, 1800–1900* (London: SPCK, 1954), pp. 92–127.

8 Amalarius was the author of one of the most widely used, and controversial, liturgical texts in the Middle Ages, *De Ecclesiasticis Officiis*. See David Jasper, *The Language of Liturgy: A Ritual Poetics* (London: SCM Press, 2018), pp. 55–9.

9 Blunt consistently gives this name to the Church in England as far back as St Augustine of Canterbury.

10 J. H. Blunt, *The Annotated Book of Common Prayer* (5th edn, London: Rivingtons, 1871), "An Historical Introduction to the Prayer Book", p. xvii.

11 Ibid., p. 206.

12 For more on Palmer and Maskell see Chapters 10 and 12. Blunt refers to Palmer as Sir William Palmer. In later life, Palmer claimed the disputed baronetcy of Wingham, Kent. He assumed the title in 1865, though it was never officially recognized. Philip Freeman (1818–75), was Archdeacon of Exeter, having been the third principal of Chichester Theological College (1846–54). Among his works was the frequently reprinted *Rites and Ritual: A Plea for Apostolic Doctrine and Worship* (1866).

13 John Elborow (1616–1767) was an Anglican cleric who wrote *A Guide to the Humble, or an Exposition on the Common Prayer* (1675).

14 John Shepherd (1759–1805) was the author of *A Critical and Practical Elucidation of the Book of Common Prayer* (1801). As a writer on the Prayer Book, he enjoyed some success, but his clerical career was modest, most of his ministry being spent as perpetual curate of the impoverished parish of Paddington, Middlesex, which he served faithfully.

15 Blunt, *The Annotated Book of Common Prayer,* p. vi.

16 Ibid., p. v.

17   Only 26 such Sealed Prayer Books have survived, mostly in cathedral libraries.

18   See further the comments of Walter Howard Frere on this "blunder" in *Some Principals of Liturgical Reform* (London: John Murray, 1911), p. 187.

19   Blunt, *The Annotated Book of Common Prayer*, p. 152.

20   Ibid., pp. 158–62.

21   Ibid., p. 200.

22   The Office of 1764 was in use when Samuel Seabury was consecrated the first bishop of the American Episcopal Church. It formed the basis for the first Communion liturgy of the American Episcopal Church.

23   Blunt, *The Annotated Book of Common Prayer*, p. 207.

24   Ibid., p. 215.

25   "And here is to be noted that such Ornaments of the Church, and of the Ministers thereof, at all Times of their Ministration, shall be retained, and be in use, as were in this Church of *England*, by the Authority of Parliament, in the Second Year of the reign of King *Edward* the Sixth." Depending on how the "second year" of Edward's reign was to be defined, this could be read as permitting vestments and ornaments allowed prior to the 1552 Prayer Book. This was a matter of great debate.

26   George Herring has written that "aspiring Ritualists ... had an invaluable tool, and the *Directorium [Anglicanum]* was to establish itself as the standard reference for the rest of the century". "Devotional and Liturgical Renewal", in Stewart J. Brown, Peter B. Knockles and James Pereiro (eds), *The Oxford Handbook of the Oxford Movement* (Oxford: Oxford University Press, 2017), p. 403. Herring does not mention Blunt's *Directorium Pastorale* or his *Annotated Prayer Book*.

27   J. H. Blunt, *A Key to the Knowledge and Use of the Book of Common Prayer* (new edn, London: Rivingtons, 1871), p. 17.

28   Ibid., pp. 21–2.

29   Ibid., p. 60.

30   Furthermore, a dictionary of religion, incomplete at Blunt's death, was finished by William Bentham and published in 1887.

1 6

The medieval roots of the Prayer Book: William George Henderson, *The York Missal* (1874); Thomas Frederick Simmons, *The Lay Folks' Mass Book* (1879)

As we have seen, in the nineteenth century, scholarly work in the Church of England on the Prayer Book and the history of liturgy was carried out almost entirely by working clergymen, many of them parish priests or members of cathedral chapters. This chapter will look briefly into the work of two such people, William George Henderson, Dean of Carlisle Cathedral, and Thomas Frederick Simmons, Rector of the united benefice of Dalton Holme in the East Riding of Yorkshire. Though little evidence now remains of their daily lives, it appears that they were friends and shared a scholarly interest in the recovery of medieval texts, both liturgical and devotional. In Simmons' case, this was directly related to his energetic participation in the Northern Convocation of York in the work of revision of the Prayer Book in the 1870s to make it fitter for the Church of the later nineteenth century.

We have seen in the work of Palmer, Blunt and others the Anglo-Catholic preoccupation with establishing the catholic continuity of Cranmer's Prayer Book with the liturgical uses of the late Middle Ages in Salisbury, York, Hereford and so on. Clearly this required a detailed and proper knowledge of these pre-Reformation texts which until the later nineteenth century were not available in reliably edited modern editions. William Maskell was one of the first to provide such texts for the wider public. Later in the century the extensive labours of the layman

Francis Dickinson[1] were making known the details of the Sarum Missal (Burntisland, 1861–83), but in this chapter we first spend a few moments with a lesser known figure, William George Henderson (1819–1905), for much of his working life a successful schoolmaster,[2] before becoming Dean of Carlisle in 1884, where he served faithfully until his death in 1905. Little evidence remains of his time in Carlisle, though the cathedral records indicate, among other things, his tireless and largely fruitless efforts to improve the cathedral library. His repeated applications for grants were met with a series of negative replies, all too familiar to the modern academic.[3] Some things, it seems, never change.

Henderson was a hardworking dean. Towards the end of his life, he complained that he was no longer able to work 16 hours a day! And much of his time was spent in editing medieval texts for the Surtees Society, founded in 1834 to publish documents relating to the ancient kingdom of Northumbria. A modern medieval scholar, who can be stinting in his praise of others, Richard Pfaff, remarks appreciatively that in his editing of the York Missal (1874),[4] Henderson "conducted an amazingly thorough search", though, Pfaff adds a little patronizingly, "he was not a professional scholar in the modern sense".[5] Indeed, it would have been difficult for him to have been so, and yet Henderson consulted seven manuscript and five printed editions of the York Missal in his edition, his comparative techniques remarkable for a self-taught scholar and liturgist. His work, certainly, was a considerable advance on the earlier editorial work of William Maskell. Henderson's manuscripts included a copy owned by the Vicar of Leeds (MS A), copies from Sidney Sussex College, Cambridge and Stonyhurst College, as well as the imposing Fitzwilliam Missal (Henderson MS E) dated about 1470 and kept in Cambridge. He also visited York Minster Library to see the great copy of the York Missal there,[6] a copy that was also consulted by his friend Simmons, as we shall see shortly.

Henderson's adept comparative reading of these multiple sources clearly indicates that he had abandoned the notion held by most scholars at that time, including Maskell and Simmons, that there was an "original" perfect copy of the York Mass awaiting discovery. He clearly understood that a missal, even in its printed form, was essentially a working book to be endlessly adapted, customized and reordered for a variety of uses: in York

Minster, in a parish church, in a monastery, or for a votive mass. In other words, Henderson was well aware that a liturgical text is part of a living process—the worship of the Church—setting in context (and perhaps even in question) the familiar observation printed at the beginning of every Book of Common Prayer in the essay entitled "Concerning the Service of the Church", that all things are subject to corruption, and that "the great diversity" of pre-Reformation liturgies was brought to a single and uniform Use by the imposed singularity of the BCP under the various Acts of Uniformity.[7] Corruption there undoubtedly, and perhaps inevitably, was, but adaptation is intrinsic to the different forms of public worship, and "uniformity" without any process of customization is a difficult ideal to maintain in public worship.[8] In fact, as the nineteenth century wore on, it was becoming clear in the Church of England that greater diversity in the liturgy of the Prayer Book was necessary, effected by such legislation as the Act of Uniformity Amendment Act, often referred to as the Shortened Services Act, of 1872, which was passed while Henderson was working on his York Missal.

Henderson's liturgical work did not end with the editing of the York Missal. A year later, in 1875, he published the *Pontificalis* of Archbishop Bainbridge of York (*c.*1462–1514). A *Pontificalis*, or Pontifical, is a medieval text providing for the particular functions of a bishop. Henderson was fully aware that this was quite a different editorial task as, unlike the almost infinitely variable forms of the Missal, the Pontifical was a book peculiar to the offices of a bishop alone, containing forms of service for the consecration of an abbot, the dedication of a church, and so on, and it actually varied very little from diocese to diocese. In the same year Henderson produced an edition of the York Manual and Processional,[9] effectively doing for the Use of York what Frere was to do for the liturgical books of Sarum a little later.[10] In fact, Henderson did himself publish his edition of the Sarum Processional in 1882, the year in which Durham University awarded him a DD.

Dean Henderson's liturgical labours have been largely forgotten, though they are given some scholarly credit by more recent medieval liturgists such as Pfaff and Matthew Cheung Salisbury.[11] But he deserves credit for his editorial work, which did much to provide material for the recovery of a living sense of liturgical development in England of which the Book of Common Prayer—Henderson's daily companion in Carlisle Cathedral—is perhaps the central part.

The same can be said of the daily life of Henderson's friend, Thomas Frederick Simmons, a parish priest to the end of his life and therefore immersed in the offices and liturgy of the BCP. It was, it seems, Simmons and not Henderson who began work on the York Missal, a task to be taken over by Henderson at an early stage. In his Early English Text Society edition of *The Lay Folks' Mass Book* (1879),[12] Simmons wrote:

> I follow the fashion of not retaining the mediaeval spelling of the Latin of the following extracts[13] though I had been very careful to do so in making my transcript some years ago, when I had undertaken to edit the York Missal, if the Surtees Society did not take it in hand. My friend Dr. Henderson has edited it for the Society, and relieved me from my engagement, to my great satisfaction, and very much to the greater advantage of liturgical students.[14]

It is clear from this that both Simmons and Henderson were developing a scholarly process that hitherto had been driven very largely by "fashion" at the hands of antiquarians. They had a sterner purpose. Simmons himself was working from only one edition of the York Missal, that in York Minster Library, and thus Henderson's careful use of multiple sources was clearly a shift in scholarly perspective, and a positive one. In addition, Simmons assumes a readership of "liturgical students". He was well aware that the EETS was essentially a secular society, and we might deduce that such "students" (as did Francis Procter in his use of the same term) were Simmons' fellow clergy as well, perhaps, as ordinands in the Church of England.

Like William Palmer, Thomas Simmons (1815–84) was from a military family, his brother General Sir John Lintorn Arabin Simmons becoming a highly distinguished diplomat/soldier and governor of the Royal Arsenal at Woolwich. Thomas was educated at Winchester College and Worcester College, Oxford, spending more than 30 years, almost his entire ministry, in the rural villages of the East Riding of Yorkshire near Beverley. During this time, he supervised the building of the magnificent church of St Mary's at South Dalton, designed in the English Gothic style by John Loughborough Pearson, the architect of Truro cathedral. Apart from his work in the parish, Simmons' major scholarly achievement was his Early English Text Society edition of the *Lay Folks' Mass Book*, a title which he himself gave to a late medieval poem in English written for the benefit of lay people attending the Latin mass. In his initial encounter with what he names as the B text of the poem, he writes that

> beside its curious ritual information, I was much struck by the fact that it was the only document I had met with that enables us to know the prayers which the unlearned of our forefathers used at mass, and by the light it threw upon their inner religious life.[15]

Although Simmons reports visits to the Bodleian Library, Oxford and elsewhere, his work is not simply a bookish exercise. He is interested in the prayers and the devotional life of the people of the Church, in both the fifteenth and the nineteenth centuries. For his editing of the LFMB is closely related to his ministry in St Mary's, Dalton Holme, and his extensive footnotes and annotations combine considerable liturgical scholarship (Simmons demands of his reader an understanding of Greek, Hebrew, Latin and German) with frequent references to his daily pastoral ministry among the latter day "lay folk" of his parish, which was certainly thriving. Reports in the Archbishop's Visitation papers of the time reveal a church at Dalton Holme that was full twice a Sunday, giving proper catechetical teaching to children and adults as required by the Prayer Book, with a surpliced choir provided with copies of *Hymns Ancient & Modern*, a hymnbook designed for use with the BCP, and engaged in extensive work with local charitable institutions in Hull and elsewhere.

Simmons' *Lay Folks' Mass Book* was a considerable achievement in scholarly terms and remains in print to the present day. The poem, in rough verse, is printed in four parallel texts, with variant readings from a further two held in Edinburgh and Cambridge. Like Henderson and the York Missal, Simmons, although he remains convinced that there is a definitive original text to be recovered—in French and from Rouen— was perfectly well aware that a written manuscript is endlessly adapted for different purposes in public worship, private prayer, monastic use

138   THE BOOK OF COMMON PRAYER AND ITS COMMENTATORS

and so on.[16] The LFMB was never printed in pre-Reformation England and underwent many permutations, clearly for different uses. All its versions are to be found in handwritten manuscripts, often embedded in collections such as the great Vernon Manuscript, written in the West Midlands dialect around 1400, and associated with a wide variety of other literature from *Piers Plowman* to recipes or books of manners.

This rich world of late medieval piety and worship, with its roots in the Latin mass, was taken up by Simmons in his often robust contributions to the newly reconstituted Northern Convocation of York[17] as it debated the revision of the BCP and its rubrics, a process that found its eventual outcome in the *Convocation Prayer Book* of 1880. This was a version of the BCP that was never authorized for use. Like most of the Prayer Book commentators whom we have met in this book, Simmons was concerned in his editorial labours with much more than simply producing a scholarly edition. He was convinced, almost certainly incorrectly, that the English poem of the LFMB could be traced back through a certain "Jeremy",[18] a priest in Cleveland who came from Rouen, to the "Gallican" liturgy of Rouen in northern France, thus helping to cement the lineage of the English liturgy in a catholic continuity that was not "Roman".[19] Although this special connection between Rouen and the English rite (particularly Sarum) has been severely questioned since the time of Edmund Bishop,[20] nevertheless, Simmons' purpose was clear: to establish the unbroken continuity of the worship of the Church of England and its Prayer Book. This he argues vigorously in Convocation, drawing on his medieval studies to guide any proposed revisions to the Prayer Book and its rubrics, and thus the public worship of the Church.

Henderson and Simmons are, in many ways, not untypical clergymen of their time, and few of their type exist in the Church of England today. Both were of a High Church persuasion, though far from being ritualists, and in their different spheres of cathedral and parish they were hard-working priests, devoted to the liturgy of the Prayer Book. They were also serious scholars, who put their learning at the service of the Church. They were convinced of the importance of studying and making more widely known the pre-Reformation ancestry of the BCP and yet they declared themselves loyal sons of the English Reformation. The records of their ministries in both Carlisle and Dalton Holme are sparse today:

a small bundle of letters and minutes of chapter meetings in the Carlisle Archive Centre for Henderson, and some parish records and archbishop's visitation papers for Simmons. Neither of them attracted a biography. But a fine memorial window in the south transept of St Mary's Church, South Dalton records Simmons' 31 years as rector of the parish as simply as possible and perhaps he would have thought that it is enough:

> To the glory of God and in memory of the Rev. Thomas
> Frederick Simmons ... also of Harriet, his wife.

Notes

[1] Francis Henry Dickinson (1813–90) was one of the founders of Wells Theological College, with an interest in liturgical history. In 1850, he published *A List of Printed Service Books, According to the Use of the Anglican Church*, before going on to edit his monumental edition of the Sarum Missal, described by Richard Pfaff as "the first modern edition of a medieval English Service Book". Richard Pfaff, *The Liturgy in Medieval England: A History* (Cambridge: Cambridge University Press, 2009), p. 9.

[2] Henderson was successively headmaster of Victoria College, Jersey and Leeds Grammar School.

[3] Correspondence to be found in Carlisle Cathedral Archives Centre, Lady Gillford's House, Carlisle, ref: DCHA/5/6/2/3.

[4] William George Henderson (ed.), *Missal ad Usum Insignis Ecclesiae Eboracensis*, The Surtees Society (Durham: Andrews & Co., 1874).

[5] Pfaff, *The Liturgy in Medieval England*, p. 451.

[6] York Minster Chapter Library, Add.30.

[7] There were in all five Acts of Uniformity, beginning in 1548, not including the Act of Uniformity Amendment Act of 1872 which, in a sense, unpicked the uniformity of the Prayer Book.

[8] Richard Gameson describes the Goldwell Missal in Durham University Library: "Corrections, additions, substitutions, multiple supplements ... and a reordering, almost all neatly done, attest to extensive use and customization of the volume, starting at an early date and continuing well into the fifteenth

century." *Literature and Devotion in Later Medieval England* (Durham: Sacristy Press, 2021), p. 87.

[9] The Manual was a book of occasional offices. The Processional was for use at litanies or processions.

[10] Walter Howard Frere, *The Use of Sarum*, 2 vols (Cambridge: Cambridge University Press, 1898, 1901).

[11] See, Matthew Cheung Salisbury, *Worship in Medieval England* (Leeds: ARC Humanities Press, 2018).

[12] For a detailed study of this, see David Jasper and Jeremy J. Smith, *Reinventing Medieval Liturgy in Victorian England: Thomas Frederick Simmons and the Lay Folks' Mass Book* (Woodbridge: The Boydell Press, 2023).

[13] That is extracts from the York *Missale* in Henderson's edition.

[14] Thomas Frederick Simmons (ed.), *The Lay Folks' Mass Book*, EETS OS 71 (London: N. Trübner, 1879), p. 354. The circumstances around why Simmons did not complete the work and why it was taken on by the Surtees Society are not known, but there seems no reason to doubt Simmons' genuine "satisfaction" at Henderson's completion of the task of editing the York Missal.

[15] Simmons, *The Lay Folks' Mass Book*, The Editor's Preface, pp. ix–x.

[16] Just how little we know of what it was like to worship in pre-Reformation England is illustrated in Nicholas Orme, *Going to Church in Medieval England* (London: Yale University Press, 2021).

[17] The York Convocation met in 1861 for the first time since it had been prorogued by Royal Writ in 1717.

[18] LFMB, Text B, line 18, p. 4.

[19] Simmons asserts firmly that "I am a clergyman of the reformed Church, and that I am one of those 'who according to the order of our Holy Reformation have deliberately and with good reason renounced the errors, corruptions, and superstitions, as well as the Papal Tyranny, which once prevailed." LFMB, p. xiv.

[20] See Edmund Bishop, "Holy Week Rites of Sarum, Hereford and Rouen Compared", in *Liturgica Historica: Papers on the Liturgy and Religious Life of the Western Church* (Oxford: Clarendon Press, 1918 [1962]), pp. 276–300.

1 7

Walter Howard Frere, *A New History of the Book of Common Prayer* (1901)

Some considerable mention has already been made of the work of Bishop Walter Howard Frere on the Book of Common Prayer in Chapter 13, in the context of his revision of Francis Procter's *History of the Book of Common Prayer* (1855). But if "Procter and Frere" was to become a familiar combination, to be found on the shelves of generations of Anglican ordinands and clergy, then a fuller account of the liturgical work of Frere must also be made, recognizing him as perhaps the last great scholar in the tradition which this book has traced from the middle years of the seventeenth century. We began with a bishop and so we shall end with one. Not only was Frere an important liturgical scholar, but he was also a significant churchman in the early years of the twentieth century leading up to the great Prayer Book debacle of 1927–8. After that, the direction of liturgical study and revision in the Church of England changed and, as the later years of the century went past, the Book of Common Prayer played a less and less central part in the worshipping life of the Church.

Walter Howard Frere was born in 1863 of a distinguished family of scholars, clergymen and politicians. His ancestor John Frere had been elected a Fellow of Gonville and Caius College, Cambridge in 1768 and was later the Member of Parliament for Norwich and Sheriff of Suffolk. In 1877, Sir Bartle Frere became Governor of the Cape Colony in South Africa. His family moved in high circles. Walter Frere gave early evidence of academic brilliance—and holiness of life. After obtaining a first class in the Classical Tripos at Trinity College, Cambridge, he moved to Wells Theological College in 1886 to be trained for ordination in the Church

141

of England. The Principal, E. C. Gibson, described him as "the most brilliant and polished scholar whom I have ever trained".[1] Frere's early interest in the Middle Ages and his passion for working from primary manuscript sources was encouraged by his cousin, Canon Christopher Wordsworth, who edited the *Sarum Breviary* in three volumes (1879–86) and the *Pontificale of St. Andrews* (1885) among many later works,[2] and was described by A. S. Duncan-Jones, Dean of Chichester, as "an accomplished antiquary".[3]

Even as a student, Frere gave evidence of a remarkable breadth of learning and attention to textual detail, though his scholarship was never dry and abstract but wholly dedicated to the living tradition of the Church's worship. As Evelyn Underhill, a close friend of his, once said, he had no taste for metaphysics. His love for the liturgical life of the pre-Reformation Church in England is shown in his early edition of the medieval offices for the use of his colleagues at Wells, *The Wells Office Book: Prime and Hours with other Services for the use of Wells Theological College* (1896, revised 1914, 1929). It was a work of considerable medieval scholarship dedicated to the service of training young men for the ordained ministry in the late nineteenth century.

Frere was throughout his life a priest dedicated to the pastoral ministry of the Church. His first five years after Wells were spent as curate of Stepney Parish Church under Edwyn Hoskyns,[4] before he became a founder member of the Community of the Resurrection with Charles Gore at Radley and later Mirfield in Yorkshire. In much demand for his preaching as a mission priest, Frere was eventually made Bishop of Truro in 1923, where he was deeply loved as a pastor and bishop. Evelyn Underhill wrote of his episcopate:

> His strong historical feeling and sense of the continuity of religion did to some extent affect the form in which his spirituality was expressed. His devotion seemed to demand embodiment, and sought it by preference in liturgic and historic forms. Hence his love of the past, his delight in the ancient Christian relics of Cornwall, and attempts to restore an interest in its saints and pilgrimages to their shrines. At confirmations he introduced the taking of a saint's name by each child confirmed; but the last

time I asked him how this had prospered he answered that it only survived in one (very extreme and troublesome) parish "where all the girls are called Joseph and all the boys are called Mary."[5]

He by no means lacked a sense of humour, and was a fine pianist with a love of music that was both ancient and modern,[6] enjoying Sir Henry Wood's often highly experimental Promenade Concerts when he had the opportunity to attend them.

Despite, or perhaps because of, his rootedness in history, Frere throughout his life was dedicated to the revision of the Church of England's Book of Common Prayer, expressing his position clearly and accessibly in his book *Some Principles of Liturgical Reform: A Contribution Towards the Revision of the Book of Common Prayer* (1911). The foundations of this book lie in his revision—one might almost say rewriting—in 1901 of Francis Procter's *History of the Book of Common Prayer* (1855), a revision which is notable not least for its substantial addition in Chapter One to the history of the Edwardine Prayer Books (1549 and 1552) and to the history of the pre-Reformation service books in England. This was undertaken because of the fact, Frere notes, that "much has been discovered and printed since Mr. Procter wrote".[7] In other words, the half century since Procter first published his book was a period of scholarly advance in the "discovery" of the liturgies and devotional literature of the late medieval English Church and the publication of modern critical editions of medieval liturgical texts, not least by Frere himself.

Frere's activities as a diocesan bishop and as a scholar did not distract him from active involvement in the politics of liturgical revision, culminating in the Prayer Book "crisis" of 1927 and 1928. At the beginning of the twentieth century, it was clear to many people, including Frere himself, that the Book of Common Prayer was in need of informed revision if it was to continue to serve the needs of the worshipping Church. Thus in 1911, Randall Davidson, the Archbishop of Canterbury, appointed an Advisory Committee on Liturgical Affairs to supervise the work of revision. Its membership was academically formidable, comprising such scholars as H. B. Swete, Christopher Wordsworth, F. E. Brightman, Percy Dearmer[8] and Frere himself. It began to address its task with liturgical precision, its first meeting in October 1912 being concerned with three questions:

- The liturgical position of Evensong on Easter Even
- The division of the Litany when followed by Holy Communion
- A proposed form of service for late Evensong.[9]

On each of these subjects, Frere wrote lengthy memoranda. But the work of the Advisory Committee proved to be ultimately frustrating. Indeed, in the years leading up to 1927, Frere found that his meticulous scholarship and suggestions were repeatedly crushed by ponderous bureaucratic procedures, liturgically ignorant bishops and the ill-informed machinery of Parliament. The compromise made in 1928 he regarded as retrograde and the resultant Prayer Book unworkable. He voted against the 1928 Prayer Book in Convocation. What is worthy of note is that a number of proposals made by Frere, such as the revision and indeed adaptation of the Psalms for congregational use, finally emerged more than half a century later in the publication of the *Alternative Service Book* in 1980.

But at the very heart of Frere's achievement in the field of liturgy is his meticulous editing of medieval liturgical texts. He has been described by Matthew Cheung Salisbury as "a textual scholar of the first order".[10] But before we briefly review Frere's major editorial achievements, a brief note on his remarkable review essay "The Palaeography of Early Medieval Music" (*Church Quarterly Review*, October 1915) is perhaps in order. First, it clearly establishes his investigations into the remote textual origins of medieval church music as based on "practical" rather than "scientific" principles. In short, this was not for him simply a technical exercise but pursued within a living tradition of music that is linked to the worship of the Church of the present day. Second, Frere develops the investigation of Enrico Marriott Bannister in his great work *Monumenti Vaticani di Paleografia Musicale Latina* (1913), which is essentially an exercise in palaeography. Picking this up, Frere notes that prior to the ninth century, in the history of plainchant, there was no clear system of notation but what he calls "neum-accents". These did not provide a system of musical intervals, and as these developed so the neum-accents fell into disuse as recognizable modern notation emerged. Frere describes this process carefully and precisely:

> For measured music the requirements which a system of notation had to fulfil were in some respects different from those which had created the system of plainsong notation. In order to meet the needs of the new music the notation must describe not a freedom of movement, but a fixity of time relationship. Consequently, the neum-accents were no longer suitable or adequate to the new task. A few survived in the "ligatures" of early mensural music: but for the most part it was the notation by points that suited best. So out of the points the "long" and the "breve" arise; and in time they are broken up into the semibreve, minim, and the smaller subdivisions of modern musical notation.[11]

This is a fine example of Frere's careful tracing of manuscript development and the meticulous scholarship that underlies his editorial work in medieval liturgy, beginning with *The Winchester Troper* (Henry Bradshaw Society, 1894), published while he was still a young curate in Stepney. Liturgy and the worship of the Church is to be undertaken with all due care and diligence and without avoidance of the hard work of proper scholarship. Anything less is tantamount to laziness.

Frere's greatest achievement as an editor was his two-volume edition of *The Use of Sarum*, published in 1898 and 1901. Volume 1 comprises the Consuetudinary (a code of customs) and the Customary (a kind of appendix to the Consuetudinary), and Volume 2, the Ordinal and the Tonal. The Introduction to Volume 1 is revealing as regards Frere's principles as an editor. He begins by noting the recent advances in knowledge of English medieval services where previously a lack of careful scholarship led antiquarians and churchmen "to have recourse to their imaginations and produce therefrom as 'correct Sarum ceremonial' much of which that illustrious church was entirely innocent".[12] Frere is perfectly well aware that manuscript copies vary and access to an "original" text is impossible, and any modern edition must therefore be in the nature of a (re)construction. First, acknowledging his debt to Canon Christopher Wordsworth, Frere recognizes the "old and persistent tradition"[13] that links the Consuetudinary as a kind of "general rubrics" for public worship with St Osmund, Bishop of Salisbury (*d.*1099), although it was perfectly clear to him that it is not actually the work of Osmund himself. Second, the name Consuetudinary is a modern and convenient title for the Sarum tractate which is described in the version that Frere calls Ms. H, *Liber et ordo de personis et dignitatibus consuetudinibus et officiis singularum personarum in ecclesia Sarum*. This was a work closely linked with liturgical practice as adopted not only in Salisbury, but also much further afield in Lincoln, Chichester, Wells and, by the early thirteenth century, even as far as Moray in northern Scotland. It was thus continually being adapted, and thus Frere sets about his task of reconstruction using four different manuscripts, two of them already well known and two at that time quite neglected.

J. H. Todd's first printed version of the Consuetudinary was published in 1846–7 using only one manuscript, called by Frere Ms. D.[14] At the same time Fr Daniel Rock was working on Ms. S for his great work *The Church of Our Fathers as Seen in St. Osmund's Rite for the Cathedral of Salisbury* (Volume 1, 1849).[15] These two manuscripts formed the basis of a further reprint of the Consuetudinary in Rich Jones' *Register of S. Osmund* (Rolls Series, Vol. 1, 1883). In addition, Frere employs two further manuscripts, which he calls H (a much later document and much enlarged) and B. The origins and descriptions of the four manuscripts are given by Frere in considerable detail. Ms. S, for example is thus minutely described:

> The scribe had his pages ruled somewhat irregularly for 32, 34, or more often 33 lines. The pages measure 10½ in. × 7½ in. the writing covering, on an average, 7 in. × 4⅜ in. (inclusive of any filling of the broad margins by insertions). The titles of the chapters are rubricated, and initials left vacant for illumination. The blank space at the end was soon filled with six or seven letters or charters, three of which have an old numbering (j–iij) in the margin.[16]

Frere uses a system of parallel texts for the Consuetudinary, while for the Ordinal in Volume 2, as a text of a liturgical rite rather than ceremonial, he uses a singular reconstruction, which he readily admits must be to a degree speculative, admitting in his Introduction the nature of the "main problem", "that is the reconstruction so far as is possible from these documents of the outline of the history of the Sarum Ordinal in the XIIIth and XIVth Centuries".[17] In short, he is consciously tracing a living tradition for the Sarum ordinal as a liturgical document that changed over a period of time and in different circumstances.

Frere's *Use of Sarum* has been criticized by modern scholars for its complexity and for being difficult to navigate. While this is true to an extent, we must nevertheless not underestimate the nature of the task which Frere set himself or the achievement of his work as an editor. Under the auspices of the Henry Bradshaw Society and with the co-operation of L. E. G. Brown, Frere also edited the *Hereford Breviary* in three volumes (1904, 1911, 1915) together with Facsimile editions (using photographs) of the Sarum Antiphonal and Gradual under the auspices of the Plainsong and Medieval Musical Society (1901–24) with a "dissertation and analytical index".[18]

This is very far from an exhaustive list of Frere's liturgical publications and editions. If at times his detailed scholarship seems rather dry and remote, all his work on medieval worship contributed to his understanding of the living, contemporary worship of the Church and its Prayer Book, which he regarded, in its 1549 form, as the culmination, if not the perfection, of an ancient tradition of liturgy within the English Church.

Thus, Frere also produced (with Percy Dearmer) an Altar Book and a Liturgical Psalter for use in church worship, and was a prolific contributor to *Grove's Dictionary of Music* (1929). Such industry and innovative editorial scholarship are all the more remarkable for a scholar who never worked within the sanctuary of a university but led a busy life as diocesan bishop, a mission priest and an active participator in the politics of Prayer Book revision in the Church of England. Perhaps it is appropriate that his last published work was peacefully entitled *The Anaphora, or Great Eucharistic Prayer: An Eirenical Study in Liturgical History* (1938).

Notes

[1] Anne Dawtry, "Walter Frere", in Christopher Irvine (ed.), *They Shaped Our Worship: Essays on Anglican Liturgists*, Alcuin Club Collections 75 (London: SPCK, 1998), p. 50.

[2] Notably, *Notes on Medieval Services in England* (1898) and (with Henry Littlehales) *The Old Service-Books of the English Church* (1904). See also p. 108, on Wordsworth's collaboration with Francis Procter.

[3] Introduction to *Walter Howard Frere: A Collection of His Papers on Liturgical and Historical Subjects*, ed. J. H. Arnold and E. G. P. Wyatt, Alcuin Club Collections XXXV (Oxford: Oxford University Press, 1940), p. ix.

[4] Sir Edwyn Hoskyns later became Bishop of Southwell. A competent biblical theologian himself, Bishop Hoskyns' son, Sir Edwyn Clement Hoskyns, translated Karl Barth's *Commentary on Romans* (1933).

[5] Evelyn Underhill and C. S. Phillips, "Spiritual Life and Influence", in C. S. Phillips and others (eds), *Walter Howard Frere: Bishop of Truro* (London: Faber & Faber, 1947), p. 180.

[6] Frere's *Historical Edition of Hymns Ancient and Modern* (1909) earned him the Cambridge degree of Doctor of Divinity in 1910.

[7] W. H. Frere, Preface to the Revised Edition of Procter and Frere, *A New History of The Book of Common Prayer* (London: Macmillan, 1905, [1949]), p. v.

[8] Henry Barclay Swete (1835–1917) was regius professor of divinity at Cambridge. Primarily a biblical and patristic scholar, he devoted much of his energies to the encouragement of theological study among the clergy. He was deeply involved in a series of Cambridge Handbooks of Liturgical Study. F. E. Brightman (1856–1932) is known primarily for his magisterial work on the BCP, *The English Rite* (1915). Percy Dearmer (1867–1936) wrote widely on liturgical and musical matters. His best-known work is *The Parson's Handbook* (1899).

[9] See R. C. D. Jasper (ed.), *Walter Howard Frere: His Correspondence on Liturgical Revision and Construction*, Alcuin Club Collections XXXIX (London: SPCK, 1954), p. 26.

[10] Matthew Cheung Salisbury, *Worship in Medieval England* (Leeds: ARC Humanities Press, 2018), p. 66.

11 W. H. Frere, "The Palaeography of Early Medieval Music", reprinted in *A Collection of His Papers on Liturgical and Historical Subjects*, pp. 98–9.

12 W. H. Frere, *The Use of Sarum*, Vol. 1 (Cambridge: Cambridge University Press, 1898), p. xi.

13 Ibid., p. xvii.

14 J. H. Todd, a fellow of Trinity College, Dublin, was presented with a copy of the Sarum Consuetudinary within the manuscript known as the Dublin Troper (now in Cambridge University Library, Add.MS 710) by Bishop Mant, subsequently publishing large portions of it in *The British Magazine* between 1846 and 1847.

15 Frere, with G. W. Hart, edited a new edition of Rock's *The Church of our Fathers* in four volumes (1903–4).

16 *The Use of Sarum*, Vol. 1, p. xliv.

17 W. H. Frere, *The Use of Sarum*, Vol. 2 (Cambridge: Cambridge University Press, 1901), p. xii.

18 These have been reprinted by the Gregg Press, Farnborough, 1966.

AFTERWORD

Towards G. J. Cuming, *A History of Anglican Liturgy* (1969)

As we have ended this book with Walter Howard Frere's *New History of the Book of Common Prayer*, so Geoffrey Cuming began his Preface to the first edition of his *History of Anglican Liturgy* (1969)[1] with a reference to Frere's work with Francis Procter. And just as Frere's revision of the work of Procter in its own time was a response to the need to revise and update the earlier work on the Prayer Book, so Cuming was responding to the need to revise and update Frere in his turn. Cuming's work is meticulous and historical; it describes at length and in detail the changes in the shape and texts of the Prayer Book offices and services over some four centuries. Rather less is said of the devotional life in the Church of England as prompted by the BCP. But it is quite simply the case that for Cuming the history of Anglican liturgy is essentially a textual history of the Book of Common Prayer since 1549. The two are more or less the same thing, and a mere 14 pages, in a book of almost 400 pages, is given by Cuming to the pre-Reformation liturgies of the English Church. At the same time, when the second edition of Cuming's book was published in 1982, the Church of England was already two years into the authorized use of its first new "Prayer Book" since 1662, the *Alternative Service Book* of 1980. So it was that Church of England priests of my own generation (I was ordained priest in Oxford Cathedral in 1977) were decreasingly familiar with the resounding cadences of Cranmer's prayers in their daily and weekly devotions, both private and public. The ASB, in its turn, has given way to *Common Worship*, while as a Scottish Episcopalian, as I am now, I worship entirely without the authority of the BCP, though its echoes remain everywhere in our worship.

150

Thus, in a sense, there can never be another history of Anglican liturgy quite like that of Geoffrey Cuming or, rather, any such history will have a different story to tell beyond the Book of Common Prayer. A few years ago, the eminent Anglican liturgist Bryan D. Spinks wrote a book entitled *The Rise and Fall of the Incomparable Liturgy: The Book of Common Prayer, 1559–1906* (2017). Whether you date the Prayer Book's "fall" as being in 1906 with the report of the Royal Commission on Ecclesiastical Discipline, or 1980 with the publication of the ASB, it is certainly true that something radical was happening in the liturgical life of the Church of England in the twentieth century. And it probably had something to do with the end of the "uniformity" (or perhaps monopoly) of the Book of Common Prayer in the public worship of the Church of England. Perhaps it was even more than that.

After the publication and authorization of the ASB, there was sometimes bitterly acrimonious criticism of the new book by many who felt that it was in the Prayer Book alone that the Church of England could find and maintain its true identity and soul. Here is a fairly typical example of that criticism found in the Introduction to a book of essays entitled *No Alternative: The Prayer Book Controversy* (1981), edited by David Martin and Peter Mullen[2]:

> It has to be admitted that the Book of Common Prayer tended to be woolly when it came to doctrines and definitions. Yet the luminous insistence of the divine presence was almost tangible. The ASB has broken the image. It has done what George Eliot said she could never do, to "lapse from the picture to the diagram." A graceless, imageless diagram it is too, a mere caricature of symbolic affirmation. When poetry is removed from liturgy what remains has something of the quality of street directions in a non-existent Kafkaesque city. It is because the ASB eschews creative theological writing that it misses the opportunity to offer a valid theological alternative.[3]

Here is not the place to re-enter a debate now almost 50 years old, though it happens that I do not agree with critics of the ASB like Martin and Mullen. That is not my main concern here. For these words are revealing of the kind of affection in which the BCP came to be held in the Church of England. They are not really theologically well informed, for the BCP is rarely "woolly" in matters of theology and doctrine, though it is often very carefully and quite deliberately ambiguous, which is quite another thing. The affection for the "poetry" of the BCP has more to do with Cranmer's extraordinary capacity to catch a tone in words—and he admitted himself that he was no poet. It is worth remembering that when the 1549 Prayer Book first appeared, its newness prompted violence and riots in the West country, the rebels comparing the Communion service to "a Christmas game", as they (like David Martin and Peter Mullen in their time) demanded the restoration of the much-loved old liturgy of the Sarum rite. With age and use comes affection and a lowering of the critical guard. The key sentence, however, relates to the almost tangible "luminous insistence of the divine presence". That, perhaps, is true, about a luminosity made stronger by loving use over a long period of time.

The BCP is a book that has been fought over, and in the wars over it people have sometimes been imprisoned (as late as the later nineteenth century), tortured and died. But it grew to be loved in its daily and weekly use, and, bathed in its words, people have been baptized, married, and died. People have been reprimanded and forgiven—or sometimes not forgiven. People have been taught by its catechism and confirmed in their faith. The sick have been comforted and souls have entered eternity on its words. Scholars and church people have argued for its place in the apostolic and catholic history of the Christian church. I hope that the essays in the present book have done something to catch that complex life and capture the importance of the Book of Common Prayer for so many people for so long.

Notes

[1] 2nd edn, 1982, which has been used for references in the present book.

[2] *No Alternative* contained essays by a number of well-known and respected writers including Rachel Trickett, C. H. Sisson, Beryl Bainbridge and Derek Brewer. Despite this its tone was unfortunate in its nastiness though less vitriolic than another collection of essays criticizing the ASB and edited by Brian Morris entitled *Ritual Murder* (1980).

[3] David Martin and Peter Mullen (eds), *No Alternative: The Prayer Book Controversy* (Oxford: Basil Blackwell, 1981), p. viii.

Further reading

The endnotes to each chapter will provide information to help the reader follow up individual authors. The following selective list is of some of the more general books that have helped me in the preparation of this book and might encourage further reading in Anglicanism and the history of the Book of Common Prayer.

Mark Chapman, *Anglicanism: A Very Short Introduction* (Oxford: Oxford University Press, 2006).

G. J. Cuming, *A History of Anglican Liturgy* (2nd edn, London: Macmillan, 1982).

Brian Cummings, *The Book of Common Prayer: The Texts of 1549, 1559, and 1662* (Oxford: Oxford University Press, 2011).

Brian Cummings, *The Book of Common Prayer: A Very Short Introduction* (Oxford: Oxford University Press, 2018).

Horton Davies, *Worship and Theology in England:*

From Cranmer to Hooker, 1534–1603 (Princeton: Princeton University Press, 1970).

From Andrewes to Baxter and Fox, 1603–1690 (Princeton: Princeton University Press, 1975).

From Watts and Wesley to Maurice, 1690–1850 (Princeton: Princeton University Press, 1961).

From Newman to Martineau, 1850–1900 (Princeton: Princeton University Press, 1962).

Charles Hefling and Cynthia Shattuck (eds), *The Oxford Guide to the Book of Common Prayer: A Worldwide Survey* (Oxford: Oxford University Press, 2006).

R. C. D. Jasper, *The Development of the Anglican Liturgy, 1662–1980* (London: SPCK, 1989).

FURTHER READING

William Marshall, *Scripture, Tradition and Reason: A Selective View of Anglican Theology through the Centuries* (Dublin: The Columba Press, 2010).

John R. Moorman, *The Anglican Spiritual Tradition* (London: Darton, Longman & Todd, 1983).

Paul Elmer More and Frank Leslie Cross (comp. and ed.), *Anglicanism: The Thought and Practice of the Church of England, Illustrated from the Religious Literature of the Seventeenth Century* (London: SPCK, 1935).

Kenneth Stevenson, *Covenant of Grace Renewed: A Vision of the Eucharist in the Seventeenth Century* (London: Darton, Longman & Todd, 1994).

C. J. Stranks, *Anglican Devotion: Studies in the Spiritual Life of the Church of England between the Reformation and the Oxford Movement* (London: SCM Press, 1961). (Chapter 6 is concerned with "Devotion based on the Prayer Book".)

Stephen W. Sykes, *The Integrity of Anglicanism* (London: Mowbray, 1978).

Index

Advisory Committee on Liturgical
Affairs (1911)   143–4
Alcuin of York   17
Allestree, Richard   28
Alliance of Divine Offices, The
(L'Estrange)   **14–20**, 111
Alternative Service Book (ASB) (1980)
1, 144, 150, 151
Amalarius of Metz   126, 131
Ambrose, St   13, 23, 43, 73, 121
Anatolius   121
Anaphora (Frere)   147
Ancient Collects and other Prayers
(Bright)   125
Ancient Hymns from the Roman Breviary
(Mant)   61, 63
*Ancient Liturgy of the Church of
England, The* (Maskell)   4, 46, 93,
99–101, 103
Andrewes, Bishop Lancelot   2, 3, 8, 48,
53, 56, 118, 126
Anecdotes of British Topography (Gough)
36, 102
Anglican   6, 25, 58, 70
Anglican Devotion (Stranks)   21, 48, 70
Anglican Canons, 1529–1947, The (Bray)
89
Anglicanism: A Very Short Introduction
(Chapman)   ix
Anne, Queen   22, 27, 47, 50
Annotated Book of Common Prayer
(Blunt)   78, **125–32**
Antiquarians   **29–38**
Apologia Pro Vita Sua (Newman)   31,
74, 78
Apostolic Constitutions   57, 58
Aristotle   85

Athanasian Creed   13, 17–18, 40, 48
Athanasius, St   13
Athelstan, King   18
Atkinson, John Christopher   111, 115
Atonement (Blunt)   124
Augustine of Canterbury, St   4, 78,
101, 107
Augustine of Hippo, St   10, 13, 23, 54
Ayton Priory (Neale)   118

Bainbridge, Archbishop Christopher
135
Baker, William J.   73, 75
Bampton Lectures   61
Bancroft, Archbishop Richard   3
baptism   94–97, 110, 128
Baring-Gould, Sabine   99
Basil, St   18, 43, 73
Baxter, Richard   48
Being Protestant in Reformation Britain
(Ryrie)   26
Bernard, St   23
Bernard of Cluny   121
Bethmont, Rémy   27, 28
Bibliographical Decameron, The
(Dibdin)   36
Bingham, Joseph   29, 30, **31–3**, 61,
79, 89
Bingham, Richard   32
Bishop, Edmund   84, 100–1, 138
Bishops' Book (1537)   63, 75
Bisse, Thomas   68
Blunt, John Henry   ix, 78, 81, 109,
124–32, 133
Blunt, John James   109, 130
Bodleian Library, Oxford   33, 34, 87,
102, 137

156

INDEX

Bonne, Sophia Mary 78
"Book of Common Prayer 1549, The"
  (Scott) 2
Book of Common Prayer—Annotated
  (Mant) **62-9**
Bowden, John William 77
Branch theory of catholicism 82, 84
Bray, Gerald 89
Bray, Thomas 54, 59
Breviary and Missal 41, 66, 73, 80
Bright, William 125
Brightman, F. E. 75, 111, 143, 148
Broderick, G. C. 103
Brown, Stewart 63, 68
Bucer, Martin 23, 44, 50, 73, 86, 90
Burton, Edward 73, 77
Butler, Bishop Joseph 54
Butler, Bishop Samuel 106
Butler, Samuel (writer) 106, 114

Calvin, Jean 50
Cambridge 7-8, 10, 14, 21, 40, 106, 117
Cambridge Camden Society 100, 104,
  117
Candida, St 78, 83
Cardwell, Edward 72, 81, **85-92**, 109
Carlisle 134-6
Caroline divines 2, 48
Catholic Emancipation 71
Cave, William 23, 27-8
Chadwick, Owen 103
Chapman, Mark ix
Character of the Rev. W. Palmer, The
  (Renouf) 82
Charles I 8, 16, 22, 27
Charles II 22, 35
Chichester 47
Christ Church, Oxford 72
Christian Initiation (Jagger) 111
Church, R. W. 72, 74, 75
Church of Our Fathers, The (Rock, rev.
  Frere and Hart) 146
Chrysostom, St John 9, 11, 17, 18, 23,
  33, 43, 73, 112
Clapham Sect 83
Clay, William Keatinge 109, 115

Clergy-Man's Vade Mecum, The
  (Johnson) 42
Clutterbuck, John 68
Coleridge, Sir J. T. 54, 59, 60
Coleridge, S. T. 31, 61
Collect for First Sunday in Lent 73, 75
Collection of Articles, Injunctions,
  Canons, A (Sparrow) 12
Collection of Offices, A (Taylor) 3
Comber, Thomas 4, **21-8**, 39, 40, 41,
  47, 48, 50, 56, 64, 109, 127
Comfortable Words 62, 129-30.
Comment on the Book of Common
  Prayer, A (Nicholls) **47-52**
Common Worship 150
Community of the Resurrection 111,
  142
Companion for the Festivals and Fasts
  (Nelson) 39
Companion to the Temple, A (Comber)
  21-8, 64
Compline vii
Concilia Magnae Britanniae et Hiberniae
  (Wilkins) **33-6**, 87
confirmation 110
Constantinople, Fifth General Council
  of 18
Convocation Prayer Book, The (1880)
  67, 112, 138
Convocations (York and Canterbury)
  67, 133, 138, 140
Copeland, W. J. 76
Corrie, G. E. 40, 45
Cosin, Bishop John 2, 48, 64, 88, 126
Coverdale, Giles 52
Court of Arches 95, 96, 97
Cranmer, Archbishop Thomas vii, 1,4,
  6, 50, 86, 110, 133
Cromwell, Thomas 52
Crosby, Benjamin 27, 69
Crutwell, Clement 57
Cuming, Geoffrey J. 1, 6, 13, 45, 69, 92,
  107, **150-1**
Cummings, Brian 37
Cyril, St 11

158 THE BOOK OF COMMON PRAYER AND ITS COMMENTATORS

Dalton Holme, Yorkshire 137
Davidson, Archbishop Randall 143
Davies, G. C. 103, 104
Davies, Horton 21, 27
Dearmer, Percy 101, 105, 143, 147
De Civitate Dei (Augustine) 11, 13
Defensio Ecclesiae Anglicanae (Nicholls) 47–8
Denison, Bishop Edward 94
Denison, G. A. 72
"Deposited Book" (1928) 5
Derby Workingmen's Association Penny Bank 125
Description of the Ivories, Ancient and Modern (Maskell) 99
Desert Fathers 79
Dibdin, Thomas Frognall 36, 38, 102
Dickinson, F. H. 102, 134, 139
Dictionary of Hymnology, A (Julian) 68, 120
Directorium Anglicanum (Purchas and Lee) 128
Directorium Pastorale (Blunt) 124–5
Directory (1644) 126
Dix, Gregory 20
Documentary Annals of the Reformed Church of England (Cardwell) 86
Donaldson, Gordon 92
D'Oyly, George 62, 67
Durandus of Mende, Bishop William 7, 10, 12, 17, 23, 117–18
Durham 22, 124
Durham Book, The 88, 92, 126
Dykes, John Bacchus 126

"Early Communion" (Scott) 5
Early English Text Society 4, 102, 108, 112, 115, 137
Easter 33
Ecclesiae Primitivae Notitia ("Blackamore") 32
Edward VI 34, 37, 87
Elborow, John 126
Elgin, Lord 71
Eminent Victorians (Strachey) 95
English Rite, The (Brightman) 111

Enquiry into the Doctrine of the Church of England, An (Maskell) 95
Epiclesis 57, 81
Episcopal Church in the USA 112
Erastianism 55, 98
Essays on Liturgiology (Neale) 119–20
Ethelbert, King 101
Explanation of the Rubrics (Mant) **64–7**

Fairfax, Lord 34
Francis de Sales, St 51
Freeman, Philip 114, 126, 131
Freemantle, W. H. 103
Frere, Bishop W. H. 4, 20, 46, 81, 91, 100, 107, 108, 110, 111, 112–13, **141–9**, 150
Froude, Richard Hurrell 72, 84
Fuller, Thomas 19
Fust, Sir Herbert Jenner 94

Gallican Use 107, 113, 114, 126
Gameson, Richard 139
Gelasian Sacramentary vii
George IV 71
Germanus, St 121
Gibson, E. C. 142
Gladstone, W. E 62
Goar, Jacques 23, 27
Goldwell Missal 139–40
"Good King Wenceslas" (Neale) 121
Goodricke, Bishop Thomas 8
Gorham, George Cornelius 94–6, 110
Gough, Richard 30, 36, 38, 79, 80, 102
Great Bible (1539) 52
Great Duty of Frequenting the Christian Sacrifice, The (Nelson) 39
Gregory, Pope 18, 43, 73, 107
Gregory of Nyssa, St 33
Grove's Dictionary of Music 147

Hackney Phalanx 77
Hammond, Henry 23, 27
Hampton Court Conference (1604) 64, 87
Härdelin, Alf 20, 91

INDEX

Harley, Sir Edward 34
Hawkedon, Suffolk 2, 7
Hawker, Stephen 99
Hearne, Thomas 34
Heeney, Brian 131
Henderson, William George 4, 102, 133, **134–6**, 137
Henry VIII 2, 41, 87, 97, 98
Henry Bradshaw Society 4, 112, 147
Herbert of Raglan, Lord 19
Hereford Breviary (Frere) 147
Herring, George 83, 132
Heylyn, Peter 14–15, 19, 35, 87
Hill, Rosemary 29, 30, 36, 37
History of Anglican Liturgy, A (Cuming) 107, **150–1**
History of the Book of Common Prayer (Procter) 4, **106–16**
History of the Church of Ireland (Mant) 62
History of Conferences and other Proceedings (Cardwell) 87–9
History of the Holy Eastern Church, The (Neale) 118
History of the Reformation (*Ecclesia Restaurata*) (Heylyn) 35
Holy Communion 43–4, 56, 57, 58, 80–1, 86–7, 90, 109–10, 128
Holy Living (1650) and *Holy Dying* (1651) (Taylor) 25
Hooker, Richard 2–3, 8, 16, 23, 64
Hoskyns, Bishop Edwyn 142, 148
Household Theology (Blunt) 130
Hymns: Ancient & Modern 121, 137
Hymns for Children (Neale) 120
Hymns for the Sick (Neale) 120

Introduction to the Devout Life (Francis de Sales) 51
Irvine, Christopher 148

Jagger, Peter 111, 115
James, Epistle of 25
Jasper, D. 6, 46, 59, 83, 131
Jasper, R. C. D. 6, 69, 76, 92
Jebb, Bishop John 63, 77

Johnson, John 42, 45
Jones, Rich 146
Julian, John 68, 120
Justin Martyr 23

Keble, John 15, 53–4, 55, 57, 59
Keeling, William 4, 6, 17
Key to the Knowledge and Use of the Book of Common Prayer, A (Blunt) 129
King James Bible 60
King's Primer, The 50
Knox, Alexander 77, 83

Lathbury, Thomas 109, 115
Laud, Archbishop William 2, 7, 14, 19, 25, 57, 88, 126
Lay Folks' Mass Book 56, 136–8
Le Brun des Marette, Jean-Baptiste 79
L'Estrange, Lady Anne 16
L'Estrange, Hamon viii, 2, 3, 4, 8, 9, 11, **14–20**, 23, 39, 40, 64, 80, 87, 108, 111, 126
Library of Anglo-Catholic Theology 15, 57, 58
Liddon, H. P. 72, 75
Life of Pusey (Liddon) 72
Life of Thomas Wilson (Keble) 53–4
Litany (1544) 50, 52
Littledale, R. F. 118, 122
Liturgiae Britannicae (Keeling) 4, 17
Liturgies of SS. Mark, James, Clement, Chrysostom, and Basil (Neale and Littledale) 118
Lloyd, Bishop Charles 39, 45, 69, **70–6**, 77, 99
Lyndwood, Bishop William 17, 20

Mabillon, Jean 101
Malines Conversations 113
Manners-Sutton, Archbishop Charles 62
Manning, Cardinal Henry Edward 95, 98, 99
Mant, Bishop Richard 46, **61–9**
Mant, Walter Bishop 67
Marshall, Peter 5

160   THE BOOK OF COMMON PRAYER AND ITS COMMENTATORS

Marshall, William   45
Martène, Edmond   101
Martiloge in Englysshe, The (Procter and
    Wordsworth)   108
Maskell, William   4, 6, 17, 36, 38, 46,
    79, 84, 91, **93–105**, 109, 111, 126,
    133, 134
Mason, J. F. A.   75
Medd, Peter G.   125, 127, 128
Medieval Hymns and Sequences (Neale)
    120
Meditation 16 on the Ordinance (King
    Charles)   8
Melanchthon, Philipp   86
Maryon, Margaret   106
Methodism   40
Milton, Anthony   19
Mirfield   107, 111, 113, 142
Moberly, George   73
Monumenta Ritualia Ecclesiae Anglicanae
    (Maskell)   94, 101–2, 103
Moravian Church   55
Morris, Richard   viii
Mozley, Thomas   78, 83
Murray, Placid   30, 37

Narrative of Events, A (Palmer)   81
Neale, John Mason   12, 113, 116,
    117–23, 127
Nelson, Robert   39, 45
Nestorian liturgies   79
*New History of the Book of Common
    Prayer, A* (Procter and Frere)   **141,
    143**
Newman, Cardinal J. H.   12, 13, 15, 20,
    30, 31, 37, 54, 72, 74, 77, 78, 81, 82,
    83, 98, 99
Newsome, David   72, 75
Nias, J. C. S.   103
Nichols, Bridget   73, 75
Nicene Creed   40
Nicholls, William   40, 45, **47–52**, 56,
    64, 109
No Alternative (eds Martin and Mullen)
    151–2
Nockles, Peter   80, 81, 98, 103, 104

Nonjurors   27, 39

Oakeley, Frederick   72
Of Religious Assemblies (Thorndike)   9,
    17, 20
Of the Laws of Ecclesiastical Polity
    (Hooker)   2, 23
On the Study of Words (Trench)   120
"Order of the Communion" (1547)   34–5
Origines Ecclesiasticae (Bingham)   30,
    31–3, 61
Origines Liturgicae (Palmer)   20, 46,
    73, 74, **77–84**, 98, 99, 100, 119
Orme, Nicholas   140
Ornaments Rubric   128, 132
Orrell, Susanna   7
Osmund of Salisbury, St   50, 52, 145
Overall, Bishop John   8, 12
Oxford   31, 33, 40, 47, 61, 71–6, 77, 85
Oxford English Dictionary (OED)   120
Oxford Movement   3, 15, 17, 30–1, 41,
    53–4, 55, 58, 63, 69, 71, 74, 77, 79, 82,
    109, 111, 117

Palmer, William   ix, 15, 20, 36, 39, 45,
    46, 73, 74, 76, **77–84**, 85, 98, 99, 100,
    101, 109, 119, 126, 131, 133
Palmer, William (of Magdalen)   118
Parson's Handbook, The (Dearmer)   101
Pearson, John Loughborough   138
Peel, Robert   71, 85
Perry, T. F.   128
Perry, Walter   126
Peter Martyr   63, 86
Pfaff, Richard W.   93, 103, 134, 135
Phillpotts, Bishop Henry   94–7
Piers Plowman (Langland)   138
Poetical Works of Thomas Warton (ed.
    Mant)   61
Polycarp, St   25
Pontificale of St Andrews   142
Pontificalis (Bainbridge)   135
Porter, W. S.   114
Prayer Book of Edward VI (1549)   1, 4,
    35, 63, 80, 81, 86–7, 90, 100, 113, 127,
    129, 143, 152

INDEX

Prayer Book of Edward VI (1552)   46, 63, 66, 81, 86–7, 90, 143
Prayer Book (1559)   11
Prayer Book (1662)   65, 87, 88, 127, 129
Prayer Book Controversy, 1927–8   113, 141, 143, 144
Present Position of the High-Church Party, The (Maskell)   96
Priest to the Altar, The (Medd)   125–6
Primers   17
Principles and Duties of Christianity (Wilson)   55
Procter, Francis   ix, 4, **106–16**, 127, 136, 143, 150
Provinciale (Lyndwood)   20
Pugin, Augustus   117
Pusey, E. B.   72, 85

Quiñones, Cardinal Francisco   6, 80

Ratcliffe, Edward C.   39, 45
Rational Illustration of the Book of Common Prayer (Wheatly)   **39–46**, 47, 51, 64, 108–9
Rationale Divinorum Officiorum (Durandus)   7, 23, 117–18
Rationale upon the Book of Common Prayer (Sparrow)   1, **7–13**, 17, 22, 26, 109
Real Presence, Doctrine of   42, 86, 88, 109, 127
Reformation, English   vii, 2, 30, 35, 41, 65, 80, 87, 113, 127
Reign of Charles I (L'Estrange)   14
Reinventing Medieval Liturgy in Victorian England (Jasper and Smith)   ix
Remains (Froude)   84
Renaudot, Eusebius   79
Renouf, Peter le Page   82, 84
Reserve, Doctrine of   78
Ridley, Bishop Nicholas   8, 35, 37
Rise and Fall of the Incomparable Liturgy, The (Spinks)   151
ritual   66, 67
Rock, Fr Daniel   146

"Roman' Catholicism"   42–3, 44, 80
Romans, Epistle to the   11
Rose, James   77
Rouen   138
Royal Commission on Ecclesiastical Discipline (1904)   5
Royal Commission on Ritual (1867–70)   126, 131
Royal Supremacy   97
Ryrie, Alec   26, 28

Sackville College, East Grinstead   119
Sacra Privata (Wilson)   53, 54, 57–8
Sacramentary of St Gregory   23
saints' days   43, 45
Salisbury, Matthew Cheung   38, 84, 104, 105, 135, 144
Sancroft, Archbishop William   22, 25
Sanderson, Bishop Robert   2
Sarum (Salisbury) Use   vii, 3, 4, 17, 23, 36, 50, 63, 73, 100, 101, 102, 108, 112, 126, 127, 133, 134, 138, 142, 145–7
(Frere), 152
Savoy Conference (1661)   35, 64, 73, 87
Scobell, John   119
Scott, David   5, 6
Scott, Sir Walter   31
Scottish Communion Office (1764)   128, 132
Scottish Prayer Book (1637)   4, 17, 19, 88, 112, 126
Seabury, Bishop Samuel   132
Sealed Books (1662)   51–2, 127, 132
Sermon Concerning Confession of Sins, A (Sparrow)   7
Shepherd, John   127, 131
Shepperton Manor (Neale)   118
Short and Plain Instruction, A (Wilson)   3, **53, 55–7**, 111
Short History of Socinianism, A (Nicholls)   47
Shortened Services Act (1872)   135
Simmons, Sir John Lintorn Arabin   136
Simmons, Thomas Frederick   ix, 4, 46, 56, 59, 69, 102, 105, 111, 112, 133, 134, **136–9**

162 THE BOOK OF COMMON PRAYER AND ITS COMMENTATORS

Simpliciad, The (Mant) 61
Smectymnuus 16, 20
Smith, Jeremy ix, 6, 46, 59, 83
Society for Promoting Christian
   Knowledge (SPCK) 55, 59, 68
Society of St Margaret 119
Sodor and Man 3, 53–60
Some Principals of Liturgical Reform
   (Frere) 143
Southey, Robert 31, 61
Sparrow, Bishop Anthony 1, 4, **7–13**,
   17, 18, 22, 23, 26, 39, 40, 64, 70, 87,
   108, 109, 111, 126
Spinks, Bryan 68, 92, 123, 151
Spurr, John 12
Stanley, William George Richard (Earl
   of Derby) 54, 55
Stapleton, Mary Harriet 71
Stevenson, Kenneth 5, 13, 56, 57, 58,
   59, 60
Stonegrave, Yorkshire 21–2, 27
Stone, Darwell 84
Stowell, Hugh 59
Strachey, Lytton 95, 103
Stranks, C. J. 21, 27, 48, 51, 70, 75
Strype, John 109
Surtees Society 102, 134–6
Swete, H. B. 143, 148
*Symbolism and Churches and Church
   Ornaments* (Neale and Webb) 12,
   117–18
Synodalia (Cardwell) 89–90

Tanner, Bishop Thomas 35, 37
Taylor, Bishop Jeremy 3, 23, 25, 28, 53,
   56, 58, 62, 64, 67
Tertullian 25
Test and Corporation Acts 71, 75
Thibodeau, Timothy M. 12
Third Collect for Evening Prayer vii
Thomas à Kempis 121
Thorndike, Herbert 9, 12, 17, 20
Thornton, Alice 21
Time's Witness (Hill) 29, 30
Todd, J. H. 146, 149
Tomline, Bishop George 64, 68

Tovey, Phillip 111, 114
Towle, Eleanor A. 121
Tractarians 12, 17, 39, 78, 93, 98, 100,
   109, 111, 113, 121, 128
Tracts for the Times 4, 41, 53, 63, 88
Transubstantiation 44
Treatise on the Church of Christ, A
   (Palmer) 81–2, 85
Trench, Archbishop Richard Chenevix
   120, 123
Trimnell, Bishop Charles 32, 37
Trinity College, Dublin 54, 77
Turner, Bishop Ashurst Gilbert 119
Two Books of Common Prayer, The
   (Cardwell) **86–8, 90**

Underhill, Evelyn 142
Uniformity, Acts of 48, 65, 135, 139
Ussher, Archbishop James 17–18

Van Mildert, Bishop William 68, 88,
   92, 112
Vatican Council, First (1869–70) 99
Vernon Manuscript 138
Vicecomes, Joseph 20
Warton, Joseph 61
Watson, J. R. 120
Watts, Isaac 55
Webb, Benjamin 12, 117
Webster, Sarah Norman 118
Wells Office Book, The (Frere) 142
Wheatly, Charles 4, 22, **39–46**, 47, 51,
   64, 70, 73, 78, 80, 101, 108–9, 111, 127
Whiston, William 60
White, James F. 118
Whiting, C. E. 27
Whole Duty of Man, The 26
Wied, Archbishop Hermann von 130
Wilberforce, Isaac 72
Wilberforce, Robert 72
Wilkins, David 29, 30, **33–6**, 79, 87,
   89, 91
William and Mary 22
Williams, George 118
Wilson, Bishop Thomas 3, 4, 6, **53–60**,
   62, 64, 70–1, 111

Wilson, W. D.   64, 68
Winchester College   61, 67
Winchester Troper, The (Frere)   145
Wingham, Kent   78
Witton, Norfolk   106, 112
Wodehouse, P. G.   19
Wood, Sir Henry   143
Wordsworth, Christopher   108, 114,
   142, 143, 145
Wordsworth, William   31, 61
Worship and Theology in England
   (Davies)   21
Wynkyn de Worde   108

Yates, Nigel   68
York Minster   vii, 22
York Use   63, 100, 102, 133, 134–6, 137

Zinzendorf, Count Nicolaus   55
Zwingli, Ulrich   90, 130

The Alcuin Club:
Promoting the Study of Liturgy

Founded in 1897, the Alcuin Club seeks to promote the study of Christian liturgy and worship in general with special reference to worship in the Anglican Communion. The Club has published a series of Annual Collections, including *A Companion to Common Worship*, Volumes 1 and 2, edited by Paul F. Bradshaw; and a new completely revised 4th edition of Jasper and Cuming's *Prayers of the Eucharist Early and Reformed*, edited by Paul F. Bradshaw and Maxwell E. Johnson (Liturgical Press 2019); also *Dean Dwelly of Liverpool: Liturgical Genius* by Peter Kennerley (Carnegie Publishing 2015), *Ancient Christian Worship* by Andrew B. McGowan (Baker Academic 2016), *The Rise and Fall of the Incomparable Liturgy: The Book of Common Prayer 1559 – 1906* by Bryan D. Spinks (SPCK 2017) and by the same author *Scottish Presbyterian Worship* (St Andrew Press 2020); *The Pilgrimage of Egeria* by Anne McGowan and Paul Bradshaw (Liturgical Press Academic 2018), *Lively Oracles of God: Perspectives on the Bible and Liturgy* edited by Gordon Jeanes and Bridget Nichols (Liturgical Press Academic 2022), *Shaping the Assembly: How our buildings form us in worship* edited by Thomas O'Loughlin (Messenger Press 2023) and *Hearing our Prayers: An Exploration of Liturgical Listening* by Juliette Day (Liturgical Press Academic 2024).

The Alcuin Liturgy Guide series aims to address the theology and practice of worship, and includes *The Use of Symbols in Worship*, edited by Christopher Irvine, two volumes covering the celebration of the Christian Year: *Celebrating Christ's Appearing: Advent to Christmas*; and *Celebrating Christ's Victory: Ash Wednesday to Trinity*, both by Benjamin Gordon-Taylor and Simon Jones, and most recently *Celebrating Christian Initiation* by Simon Jones.

The Club works in partnership with the Group for the Renewal of Worship (GROW) in the publication of the Joint Liturgical Studies series, with two studies being published each year.

In 2013 the Club also published a major new work of reference, *The Study of Liturgy and Worship: An Alcuin Guide*, edited by Juliette Day and Benjamin Gordon-Taylor (SPCK 2013).

Members of the Club receive publications of the current year free and others at a reduced rate. The President of the Club is the Rt Revd Dr Stephen Platten, its Chairman is the Revd Canon Christopher Irvine, and the Secretary is the Revd Thomas McLean. For details of membership and the annual subscription, contact: The Alcuin Club, 20 Burrows Close, Headington, Oxford OX3 8AN United Kingdom; email: publications@alcuinclub.org.uk; or visit the Alcuin Club website at: www.alcuinclub.org.uk.

EU GPSR Authorized Representative:

LOGOS EUROPE, 9 rue Nicolas Poussin, 17000 La Rochelle, France

contact@logoseurope.eu

www.ingramcontent.com/pod-product-compliance
Ingram Content Group UK Ltd.
Pitfield, Milton Keynes, MK11 3LW, UK
UKHW021009260525
458805UK00003B/3